The
KATE WOLF
SONGBOOK

The
KATE WOLF
SONGBOOK

Editor
Max Wolf

Project coordinator and book design
Beth Weil

Business and editorial assistance
Terry Fowler

Editorial assistance
Hannah Wolf

Another Sundown Publishing Company
San Francisco, California

For songbook, concert video, record, cassette and compact disc
ordering information write to:

Owl Productions
P.O. Box 151208
San Rafael, CA 94915-1208

Kate's companies, Another Sundown Publishing Co. and Owl Productions, are managed by her children, Max and Hannah, and her widower, Terry Fowler.

The design for the Medicine Wheel following the Table of Contents is from Sun Bear's vision. Information about the Medicine Wheel is available from the Bear Tribe, Box 9167, Spokane, Washington 99209. This design is used by permission.

Photography Credits

Lloyd Barde   75, 83
Ron Blanchette   Frontspiece Back Roads, 17, 20, 25, 43, 46,
        81, 97, 126
Victor Budnik   115
Morrie Camhi   23
Roseann Carcello   67
Susan Casey   Title
Dwight Caswell   33
Paul Coates   92
Mansel Davies   113
Lee Davis   41
Peter Fisk   9
Terry Fowler   63
Raimon RP Franck   27, 77
Nina Gerber   91, 95
Pat Goudvis   65
J.P. Greenwood   19
Mariah Healy   73
Beth Jones   103

Robert Kyle   127
Harriet Lewis   105
Karl Metzenberg   Cover, 11, 13, 15, 37, 51, 68, 119, 140
Fred Mertz   107
Peter Novak   101
Jaime O'Neill   121
Pomeroy S.F.   80
Art Rogers/Pt. Reyes   110
Jack Ruch   103
Randy Sabien   117
Beth Weil   131
Nicholas Wilson   53
Kate Wolf   71, 109
Max Wolf   123, 129
Saul Wolf   3, 7
Jay Yarnall   89

Published by
  Another Sundown Publishing Company
  San Francisco, California
All songs published by Another Sundown Publishing Company (BMI) except:
  The Redtail Hawk George Schroder, ©1975 Gratitude Music Co. (BMI). Used by permission.
All songs written by Kate Wolf except:
  Everybody's Looking For The Same Thing Kate Wolf & Hugh Shacklett
  Friend Of Mine Lyrics: Kate Wolf; Music: Kate Wolf, Nina Gerber & Ford James
  The Redtail Hawk George Schroder

Library of Congress Card Catalog Number 87-70899
International Standard Book Number 0-9618706-0-5

Music typesetting by Mansfield Music-Graphics,
Oakland, California.

Fifth Printing June 1993
McNaughton & Gunn, Inc.
Ann Arbor, Michigan

Dedicated to
Kate Wolf
January 27, 1942—December 10, 1986

ACKNOWLEDGEMENTS

Many thanks to:

Nina Gerber and Bill Griffin for their intimate familiarity with Kate's
    music
Tom Diamant and Jeff Alexson of Kaleidoscope Records for their caring
    interest in the future of Kate's music
Bruce "Utah" Phillips for sharing his memories with us
Sarah Phoenix for invaluable advice
Janet Smith for her help and interest
The many photographers who let us use their photos of Kate and those
    photographers whom we couldn't reach or identify
Thanks most of all to Kate's fans who gave her the encouragement
    and support to achieve the works that constitute this songbook

INTRODUCTION

This collection contains the fifty-six songs that Kate wrote (two are co-authored) and recorded for her albums. Kate contemplated this book for years, but never found the hours to sit down and work on it. However, she spoke with family and friends about how she wanted to approach this project, and we have tried to carry these thoughts through to the book's completion. This process was difficult and slow—folk music speed—but very interesting.

A few words regarding the songbook's structure. Songs are listed by album chronologically—if you can't find a particular song, consult the discography or alphabetical index at the back of the book. Four songs that Kate re-recorded live for her *Give Yourself To Love* album are placed with the original earlier albums. Kate's seventh album, *Gold In California:* contains only previous recordings of her songs (see discography). Kate recorded songs written by friends and colleagues that have become familiar as "Kate Wolf songs." Her favorite, *The Redtail Hawk,* a concert-closing signature song, is included here.

Many of Kate's fans are not just listeners but musicians also. Kate knew her songbook would be used by livingroom guitarists and early morning melody makers, and we've designed this book with them in mind. Songs are usually presented in their basic forms, without recorded arrangements or harmony parts. Each song is written in the key it would be played out of on the guitar. For example, if a song was recorded in F and Kate played it out of a D chord, with a capo on the 3rd fret, the song is written in D. Transposing may be necessary for other instruments or for singers with vocal ranges different from Kate's. Kate was for the most part a singer and songwriter and not a complex guitar player. Her chords were mostly basic configurations of standard chords that can be found in any guitar chord book. However, she occasionally used a complex chord that is integral to the playing of the song. These chords are graphed on page 133.

Kate began to write songs in 1971, and produced over 200 works in fifteen years. Many exist only on old tapes recorded in various livingrooms, while others never went further than the back of an envelope. She recorded most of her favorites, but had to omit many others; a situation similar to this songbook. Several of Kate's unreleased recordings are being compiled for future albums, and a possible second songbook would contain this new music along with songs we couldn't include here. We hope you find this songbook useful, entertaining and worthwhile.

Bruce Utah Phillips and Kate

RECOLLECTIONS
MIRRORS AND WINDOWS
Reflections and Observations
by
Bruce "Utah" Phillips

"The songs I write stop time, just like photographs, and let me look at the moments of our lives. A lot of songs I write take those moments, and they're either mirrors or windows." Kate Wolf said that, and no one's ever said it better. Now all it takes is the courage to look into the mirrors or out of the windows, I mean really *look* and try to be honest about what you see there. Kate held up a lot of mirrors for me to look at, and I tried to open a few windows for her. It was a fair trade. Kate again, "When I went on tour with Bruce Phillips there was a balance. There was a real interesting contrast. I think we each filled in the other's half. He's a little gun-shy about being quite so personal as I am, and I'm gun-shy about being so political as he is." And *there* was the touchstone.

On that tour, Kate's first in the East, I was invited to sing at a Karen Silkwood rally in a little park behind the White House. On the way down to Washington, somewhere below Baltimore, Kate asked me to describe the kind of affair we were going to. I rummaged in my kit and passed back the flyers and newsletters I had received from the Oil, Chemical and Atomic Workers Union. An hour later we were at the rally and, after I sang, Kate asked if she could sing too. The organizers were delighted. Kate walked up to the mike and taught the crowd one of the best singalongs I've ever heard; "Links In The Chain." Seems that's what she had been doing for the past hour or so in the back seat of the car, digesting the information and making up that song.

The other side of the proposition, the mirror side, was a little harder for me. No, it was a lot harder. Kate knew that I had been using Utah as a metaphor for a lot of Bruce's problems for years. When Utah spoke of labor history, "You can't know where you're going unless you know where you came from," part of that was me still grappling with my father's leaving when I was five and my leaving when my son was five. I wrote out my feelings about that once in a poem called "He Never Said Goodby." Kate found it and said, "I'll put a tune to this if you promise to sing it." I said, "Dammit, Kate, NO! Sometimes I write these things to get them out of myself, not into myself. Like dropping a bag of garbage off a cliff. Then, years later, some yahoo walks up, hands you that bag of garbage and says, 'Did you lose something?' NO! Now leave me alone." "Wait a minute," Kate said. "A lot of men go through this and a lot of men do this but never talk about it. Now here's your chance and not just for yourself either." So, she made the poem into a song, and yes, I do sing it. You see what I mean? Mirrors and windows: " . . . we each filled in the other's half." Now, with her quiet, sensible pushing, I am growing closer to owning both halves, and it feels good. Thanks, Kate.

Traveling? Kate was a far traveler, down the road and back again. But there was always time for stops to explore the odd quirky little things scattered out along the way that she refused to let pass notice, the "dancing chickens" of America. Traveling with a strong, calm, *organized* (and I mean organized) companion who also drives like she invented it makes the road fun. But doing it with an Earth-instructed, *noticing* person is the most fun I can imagine. There she is, 200 miles since daybreak and cruising, munching big lizard skins of kelp for her thyroid, meditation tapes smoothing the wrinkles, anticipating the masseuse arranged for up ahead. I'm in the other seat trying to push a story told while driving yesterday into the song she insisted it ought to be. Suddenly, there's a small road sign half hidden by the bushes: "Talking Duck Ranch." Here I thought she was lost in a road trance but no, we're turning, what the hell, gonna be late, time out, pass the kelp.

Once in town, Kate already knows where the whole-food store is. Nuts and grubs and then off to be roundly pummeled by a kind-handed stranger. Kate took care of herself. The object, it seemed, was to get back home after a long trip feeling better than when you left, not depleted or exhausted, but elated, full of excitement about places seen and lives passed through. Kate also understood that the best way to take care of yourself is to take care of the people around you. She did that simply as a matter of course, like breathing.

On stage several years ago I wrote this for a local paper in anticipation of one of her visits.

" . . . They know these songs are about them, hard-working folks falling in and out of love, jobs, politics, booze and poetry. Refugees, hill poets, bush prophets, herb growers, prospectors, no prospects, government agents, strong men and strong women weak in their strength and strong in their weakness, all of 'em some mother's child, just like you and me. And now she's here, singing to us, right up there on the stage.

This is no winsome thrush come to break your heart one more time. No angry harridan, hardened and embittered by all the road years. Oh no, not Kate. Just a woman—I mean a *woman*—straight ahead, solid, graceful, calm, working from her middle, honest as wildflowers and pretty as a new gold watch.

Ten minutes later everyone in that crowd, rolled and mugged by the entire Second Industrial Revolution, knows exactly how they want it all to turn out. The songs roll past like wind ruffling the sweet grass, pause as though deep in thought, and then burst with the passion of thunderheads roiling the summer sky. But always—*always*—kind. Two hours and a lifetime later, those good folks—warm inside, reluctant to break the spell of enchantment—will struggle back up the mountain, re-telling the stories, humming the songs, the kids dozing in a half-dream of 'Trumpet Vine' or 'The Golden Rolling Hills Of California.' They have been to an *event!*"

Whew! Now that's a lot to say about anybody. But I've seen it happen. From California to New England I've watched and listened to Kate Wolf move into people's lives, make a place for herself like family, push aside the Top 40 madness and really talk turkey.

Kate learned how to make her own life making her own music. She learned how to forgive and how to seek forgiveness. And she did it all by making friends instead of leaving a trail of bodies behind her. Kate owned what she did, shared it with all of us, laughed at herself and kept her children part of her life. Most of all, Kate always paid attention to what people were thinking and feeling. That's where the good songs come from.

Now, Kate, songmaker, poet, singer and friend has gone on. I have no statistics nor have I cared to pursue any. She was an excellent human being: her music was a bonus. Kate took care of all of us; she paid attention to us, our troubles, our confusions; she held us all in some calm center which refused to let any of us vanish. She was a healer who, through remembrance, will continue to heal, to care for us. Those of us, the traveling nation, who follow the craft of song and story were honored by her comradeship. Kate pursued an abundant life through often overwhelming hardship. But she never became embittered by that hardship; she put it to work. Kate could walk into the heart of her pain, embrace it and walk back out filled with a calm and beautiful strength which she transformed into songs of great courage, comfort and forgiveness. Throughout her life, Kate gave herself over to things of the spirit, always trying to increase her spiritual reach. Many of us delighted in watching this, too lazy or confused to try and keep up. She was always one step ahead of us anyway. She still is.

BIOGRAPHY

by Jamie Keller and Max Wolf

Kate Wolf was born Kathryn Louise Allen in San Francisco on January 27, 1942. Called Katie Lou as a child, her name was shortened to Kathy, and later to Kate. Kate's family moved around and she spent her early childhood in Oregon and Michigan, finally returning home to Berkeley where she went to school from the sixth grade through high school.

When Kate was 19, she met Saul Wolf, a UC Berkeley architecture student. Two years later they were married. Kate and Saul had two children, Max, born in 1964, and Hannah, born in 1967.

As a child, Kate was always thinking of music, and she began her musical training at the age of 4 with piano lessons from her grandmother. She played until she was 16, but stopped in high school because she felt shy and self-conscious. Even though she no longer played, Kate was strongly influenced by the music she had heard.

"I have to say that it probably started with the Weavers and led to Rosemary Clooney. I started out with singers that you could hear the words. Then I got into writers. Dylan is a big influence and of course the Beatles happened and folk music was always kind of there in the background. I got interested in folk music out of the Kingston Trio stuff and the Weavers. I wanted to know more about it, and started going to libraries. Then I discovered the Carter family. When I got into country music radio, I started to discover Merle Haggard and Lefty Frizell, and people like that. I used to listen to Hank Williams as a kid, so it's been kind of a progression through honest songs and honest singers; that kind of clarity. I guesss it's that heart that's out there."

When she was 27, Kate met some people in Big Sur on the California coast who played music in their living rooms. Kate began playing with them, and hearing their songs, realized that expressing her own thoughts to music seemed the next natural step. She was strongly influenced by her friends Gil "Jellyroll" Turner and George Schroder (*The Redtail Hawk*) who told her "Anyone can write a song. Just sit down and sing your conversations."

Kate listened to his words, and within six months she knew she was going to leave San Francisco and her family to pursue a career in music. She and her husband parted amiably, and in 1971 Kate moved to Sonoma County where she lived in her '57 Chevy for six months. She became a weekend mother, and secured a job at the Sebastopol Times Newspaper. She also performed once a week at a local bar and continued her songwriting.

Soon after, her children came to live with her. She became involved in their schooling while continuing to play music once or twice a week in a small restaurant. This went on for a couple of years, and then as Kate put it, "magical things began to happen." Performing became increasingly important to her, and she formed her first band, The Wildwood Flower with Don Coffin whom she later married. The Wildwood Flower played all kinds of community benefits, and Kate became interested in radio. She began a show on KVRE called *Uncommon Country*, and later moved to KSRO and hosted the *Sonoma County Singers Circle*.

Her Sonoma County music shows brought her new recognition, and she was offered funding for an album. With her knowledge of independent labels and the advice of record industry friends, she formed her own record company, Owl Records. *Back Roads*, her first record was made for the people of her community, and featured eight of her songs and four by other artists whose works she felt should be recorded. The next year, Kate recorded *Lines on the Paper* and went on her first tour of California.

With the release of the albums, her audience started coming out to hear the music.

"A big shift occurred where people wanted to hear my songs. It was amazing. It just kind of made its own way. They dragged us out of Sonoma County down into the Bay Area, and then we got airplay, and we started traveling further and further."

Kate's national touring began in 1977 with trips throughout the Midwest and Northwest. Her long-time friend Bruce "Utah" Phillips helped plan a tour back East where she played concerts and performed at the Philadelphia Folk Festival. Kate's love for Canadian folk music brought her even greater recognition as she performed at the popular festivals in Calgary, Winnepeg, and Vancouver. Closer to home, Kate organized the successful Santa Rosa Folk Festival.

1979 saw a change in the band and in Kate's life. Her separation with Don ended the Wildwood Flower, but saw the addition of Nina Gerber, a very talented guitar and mandolin player who would be her accompanist throughout the rest of Kate's career. Although Kate continued to publish her songs through her own company, Another Sundown Publishing, she became too busy to release records on her own label. Her first studio album, *Safe at Anchor*, was produced and released by Kaleidoscope Records, an established, independent label owned by two friends, Tom Diamant and Jeff Alexson, who had distributed Kate's previous two albums. Kate co-produced this album with Bill Griffin, her long-time friend and musical collaborator.

In the Eighties, Kate continued to tour throughout the United States. Although her popularity grew, her concerts never lost their intimacy. Whether she was playing to 500 people in a music hall, or 85 in a coffee house, her audience felt as if she had touched each one of them individually. Her music always had a strong impact on those who heard it. Fans would tell her that she was writing just what they were feeling.

"Sometimes we just can't find the words, but we all have those same feelings. You feel these things, and you don't think it's OK to say them, or you can't quite get the words, and then it comes, and it's just this breaking loose, you have a way to say it."

Kate's fourth album, *Close to You*, was released in 1981. This record was co-produced by Bill Griffin and Tom Diamant, and, like *Safe at Anchor*, featured only original compositions. In 1982 Kate married again, this time to Terry Fowler, the owner of a natural foods distribution company. She continued to perform both at concerts and at benefits for groups such as SEVA, No Nukes, and Big Mountain. In 1983 she toured the Southwest with the Academy Award winning documentary film *The Four Corners: A National Sacrifice Area?*

As her popularity grew, so did critical recognition, and twice she was nominated for best folk singer at the San Francisco Bay Area Music Awards (Bammies). Kate's favorite medium was the stage, and in 1982 and 1983 she realized her desire to record a live album, a two record set entitled *Give Yourself to Love*. The title song, written for a friend's wedding, became Kate's most popular work, and the record received the "Best Folk Album of 1983" award from NAIRD, The National Association of Independent Record Distributors and Manufacturers.

Late in 1983, following the release of *Give Yourself to Love*, Kate decided to take a year off from performing. She wanted to rest, evaluate her life, and spend more time with her family.

"The road is wearing me down. I feel my health slipping . . . For twelve years I had been moving fast and furious with my career, so I thought it was time to take a sabbatical."

During her sabbatical, she worked part-time as a production artist for the Point Reyes Light newspaper. She also studied massage and planned activities at the San Geronimo Community Center in west Marin. Kate did limited performing, but it was not publicized.

Toward the end of the year, Kate realized how important her music was to her and began performing again. She appeared on American Public Radio's *A Prairie Home Companion* in late 1984, and made frequent trips to the East Coast, especially the Washington D.C. area. After touring the Northwest in early 1985, she began working on her next album, *Poet's Heart*. Mid-1985 saw her back on *A Prairie Home Companion*, this time in San Francisco.

In the fall, Kate embarked on her final tour. She spent two weeks on the East Coast playing from Boston to Florida, and then flew to the Midwest and toured through Michigan, Wisconsin and Minnesota.

Following a brief respite at home, she flew to Texas for a taping of *Austin City Limits*. The show was aired frequently the following year, giving Kate her greatest national exposure. After performing around Texas, Kate came home and played the last leg of her tour through Southern California. *Poet's Heart*, also co-produced and arranged by Bill Griffin, was released the following January, and was awarded NAIRD's "Best Folk Album of 1986."

In April, Kate was diagnosed with acute leukemia and underwent chemotherapy at the University of California Medical Center in San Francisco. After recovery and full remission, she returned home and compiled a retrospective of her recordings. As the news of her illness spread, she received support from fans and friends all over the country. Remembering how much Kate had given of herself to the causes and people she believed in, her friends and fellow musicians organized numerous concerts to benefit Kate in her time of need.

In September, Kate reentered the hospital for a bone marrow transplant. She was feeling strong and confident, but complications from the operation destroyed her immune system and she never recovered. The 10-year retrospective album *Gold in California* was released in January 1987. The following spring, Kate Wolf became the first musician inducted into the NAIRD Independent Music Hall of Fame.

"I live for a sense of a feeling of purposefulness in this world, you know, that I could stop my life at any point and feel that my life has been worthwhile; that the people I've loved and my children have all reached a point where their lives are now going to come to fruit. And as far as something I live by, it's to try to be as alive as possible and feel free to make my mistakes and try to be as honest as I can with myself."

TABLE OF
CONTENTS

1

BACK
ROADS

Lately

Key: D
No Capo

Words & Music
by Kate Wolf

Verse:

Late - ly in the af - ter - noon I'm cry - ing o - ver you 'Though

ev - ery - thing still seems just the same And

late - ly there've been ques - tions in this heart of mine That

don't bring an - y an - swer but pain And

Hon-ey___ I can't tell if it's you or me Or

both of us that need to change And

if I thought that you could see it too

2

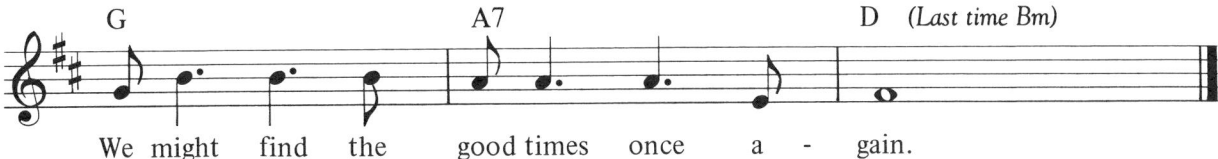

We might find the good times once a - gain.

Lately in the afternoon I'm crying over you
Though everything still seems just the same
And lately there've been questions in this heart of mine
That don't bring any answer but pain.

Chorus: And Honey, I can't tell if it's you or me
         Or both of us that need to change
         And if I thought that you could see it too
         We might find the good times once again.

Lately in the morning I love to be alone
With the words that come into my mind
And lately you've been seen coming into your own
But what is it that you're trying to find?

Chorus:

And lately in the evening I'm feeling better too
Though there's still a lonely feeling down inside
And lately I've stopped listening to all the kind advice
The way is getting clearer all the time

Chorus:

Emma Rose

Words & Music
by Kate Wolf

Key: A
No Capo

Verse:

When Em-ma Rose_ was ten years old, her fa-ther passed a-way. She
cried to think he'd nev-er see her on her wed-ding day. And
then her moth-er sick-ened_ and left her on her own, Say-ing
"Em-ma Rose it grieves me to leave you so a-lone."

Chorus:

(Tell me) How long,___ how long will it be 'til you're re-
turn-ing? How long, how long, must I___ keep the can-dles burn-ing?

When Emma Rose was ten years old, her father passed away
She cried to think he'd never see her on her wedding day
And then her mother sickened and left her on her own
Saying "Emma Rose, it grieves me to leave you so alone"

Chorus: How long, how long, will it be til you're returning?
         How long, how long, must I keep the candles burning?

When Emma Rose was sixteen years she was courted and wed
By Danny Jay the neighbor boy, a fine young man they said
And in the flowering of their love, Emma had a son
And Danny left one morning before the rising of the sun.

Chorus: Tell me . . . .

The years went by and Emma Rose grew bitter in her grief
Of all the men who came and went, none gave her any peace
And even age could not erase the beauty in her face
But Emma Rose had eyes for one who left without a trace

Chorus:

Emma lives alone now, the child is grown and gone
Some say they see her now and then on the days she comes to town
If you're traveling north, there's a mailbox on the road
And all it says is Emma Rose in letters faint and old

Chorus:

Emma Rose, Kate and Pete Wiseman at Back Roads Release Party

Sitting On The Porch

Key: A
Capo: 2nd fret

Words & Music
by Kate Wolf

Lively
Verse:

Sung one octave higher

Up be-fore the dawn, watch-ing_ the sky   Wait - ing_   for ev-ery-thing to   wake

No-tic-ing   the clouds mov-ing_   a-long   Don't you know a fine day's a-bout to break   well now

Chorus:

Can't you feel the sun and can't you feel the day Don't you know ev-ery-thing's gon-na be   O. -

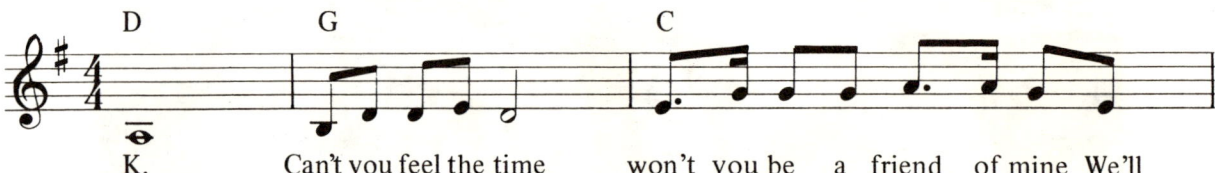

K.   Can't you feel the time   won't you be   a   friend   of mine We'll

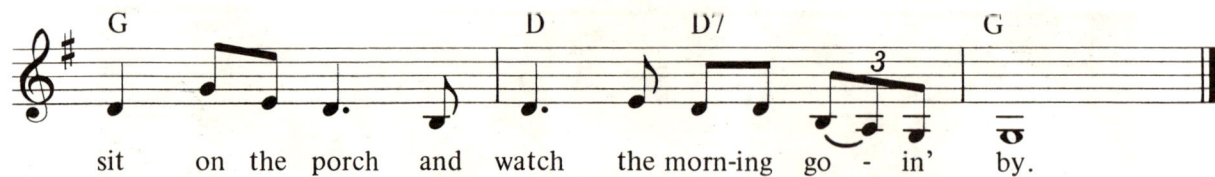

sit   on the porch   and   watch   the morn-ing go - in'   by.

6

Up before the dawn, watching the sky
Waiting for everything to wake
Noticing the clouds moving along
Don't you know a fine day's about to break

  Chorus: Can't you feel the sun and can't you feel the day
             Don't you know that everything's gonna be OK
             Can't you feel the time and won't you be a friend of mine
             We'll sit on the porch and watch the morning going by.

There's nothing I'd rather do than sit right here with you
Watching the morning going by
Singing country songs, now won't you sing along
Don't you know it's a fine way to get high

  Chorus:

We may not be here long, the night is bound to come
And who knows what roads we have to choose
But you know that when our morning comes again
We can meet here and celebrate the news

  Chorus:

The Redtail Hawk

Key: Am
No Capo

Sung one octave higher

Words & Music
by George A. Schroder

The Redtail Hawk writes songs across the sky
There's music in the waters flowing by
And you can hear a song each time the wind sighs
In the Golden Rolling Hills of California
In the Golden Rolling Hills of California

It's been so long, love, since you said goodbye
My cabin's been as lonesome as a cry
But there's comfort in the clouds drifting by
In the Golden Rolling Hills of California
In the Golden Rolling Hills of California

A neighbor came today to lend a hand
He saw I'd fixed the road as best I can
But there's just some things that need a man's hand
In the Golden Rolling Hills of California
In the Golden Rolling Hills of California

Goodbye Babe

Key: E
No Capo

Words & Music
by Kate Wolf

Verse:

My life keeps chang-ing like a clou - dy day.

You brought me sun-shine_ a - long the way. Now I

find our love is fad - ing like the ear - ly morn - ing light So

I've made up my mind to say good - night

Chorus:

Good-bye_ Babe, I___ know you'll do fine. We had

ev - ery - thing go-ing___ ex - cept e-nough time. We

nev - er were to - geth - er long e-nough to know

How we might have made it or

where we would go So Good - bye

My life keeps changing, like a cloudy day
You brought me sunshine along the way
Now I find our love is fading like the early morning light
So I've made up my mind to say goodnight

   Chorus: Goodbye Babe, I know you'll do fine
               We had everything going, except enough time
               And we never were together long enough to know
               How we might have made it or where we could go, So Goodbye

And there's nothing else, Honey, that I can do
Except to tell you I once loved you
And we'll make better friends, than lovers
And in trusting me, you might trust another

   Chorus: Goodbye Babe, I know you'll do fine
               We had everything going, except enough time
               And we never were together long enough to know
               How we might have made it or where we could go, So Goodbye

Kate at KVRE Santa Rosa 1977

Tequila & Me

Key: G
No Capo

Words & Music
by Kate Wolf

Verse:

G ... C

The tel - e - phone's ring-ing.___ the ra - di - o's sing - ing___ A

D7 ... G

song I know much too well I

G ... C

pick up the phone, here all a - lone. Who's

D ... D7 ... G

call - ing? I real - ly can't tell.

Chorus:

C

"Hel - lo___ out there you know I was just think - ing___ a -

G

bout you and I thought I would call." But

Em ... C

he can't see, it's Te - qui - la and me

12

Spend - ing   the   night   with   the   walls.

The telephone's ringing, the radio's singing
A song I know much too well
As I pick up the phone, here all alone
Who's calling, I really can't tell

  Chorus: "Hello out there, you know I was just thinking
             About you and I thought I would call"
             But he can't see, it's Tequila & Me
             Spending the night with the walls

And I figure he's thinking how far I've been sinking
And I can't say I really care
Cause I'm here all alone, with the walls and the phone,
Drinking my way to somewhere

  Chorus:

Tequila's my friend, she comes now and then
To stay til the long night is through
There's more where she came from, more of the same one
That's more than I can say about you.

  Chorus:

Riding In The Country

Key: C
No Capo
Verse:

Words & Music
by Kate Wolf

Sung one octave higher

Go-ing rid-ing in the coun-try in a Mod-el A Ford Past the cows and the

chick-ens, through the fields of corn. Out a-cross the flat-lands and the roll-ing

hills Feel the sum-mer sun shin-ing, hear the mo-tor purr.____ And I'm just

sit-ting on the front seat with two friends of mine.

Go-ing to the coun-try sure____ makes me feel__ fine.____

14

Going riding in the country in a Model A Ford
Past the cows and the chickens, through the fields of corn
Out across the flat lands and the rolling hills
Feel the summer sun shining, hear the motor purr

  Chorus: And I'm just sitting on the front seat with two friends of mine
                Going to the country sure makes me feel fine

Working in the country, cleaning up yards
With a Model A truck you know it can't be hard
Folks smile and pass up, walking down the road
Going to the county dump with another load

  Chorus:

Hayfields are cut, harvest has begun
Riding through the orchards in the morning sun
Good times in the country, can't you smell the air
Apples and apricots and plums to spare

  Chorus:

Down gentle roads with no white line
Like a pathway to another time
Old houses passing, frontyards of flowers
I could ride in the country for hours and hours

  Chorus:

Kate with Moose and Cody

Oklahoma Going Home

Words & Music
by Kate Wolf

Key: Em
No Capo

16

Another time I'm going home
Down this road on my own
I see the trees and feel the sun
Is this the time my traveling's done?

  Chorus: But Daddy, it's been too long
              Since I've been grown and gone along
              How're you doing, and how've you been?
              It'll be awhile til I'm here again.

I see the house and the old wood shed
I wonder how many friends are dead
Have you seen my boy, is he growing tall?
How's his ma, is she pretty still?

  Chorus:

The years have been good; I could be drinking less
Out on the coast I've found it's best.
There's been lots of singing and lots of pain
But you know I'd live it again.

  Chorus:

Some things haven't changed, way out there
I still have my shotgun and my long hair
And the mountains and me are the best of friends
I'm still looking for a woman that really understands

  Chorus:

Back Roads

Key: G
No Capo

Words & Music
by Kate Wolf

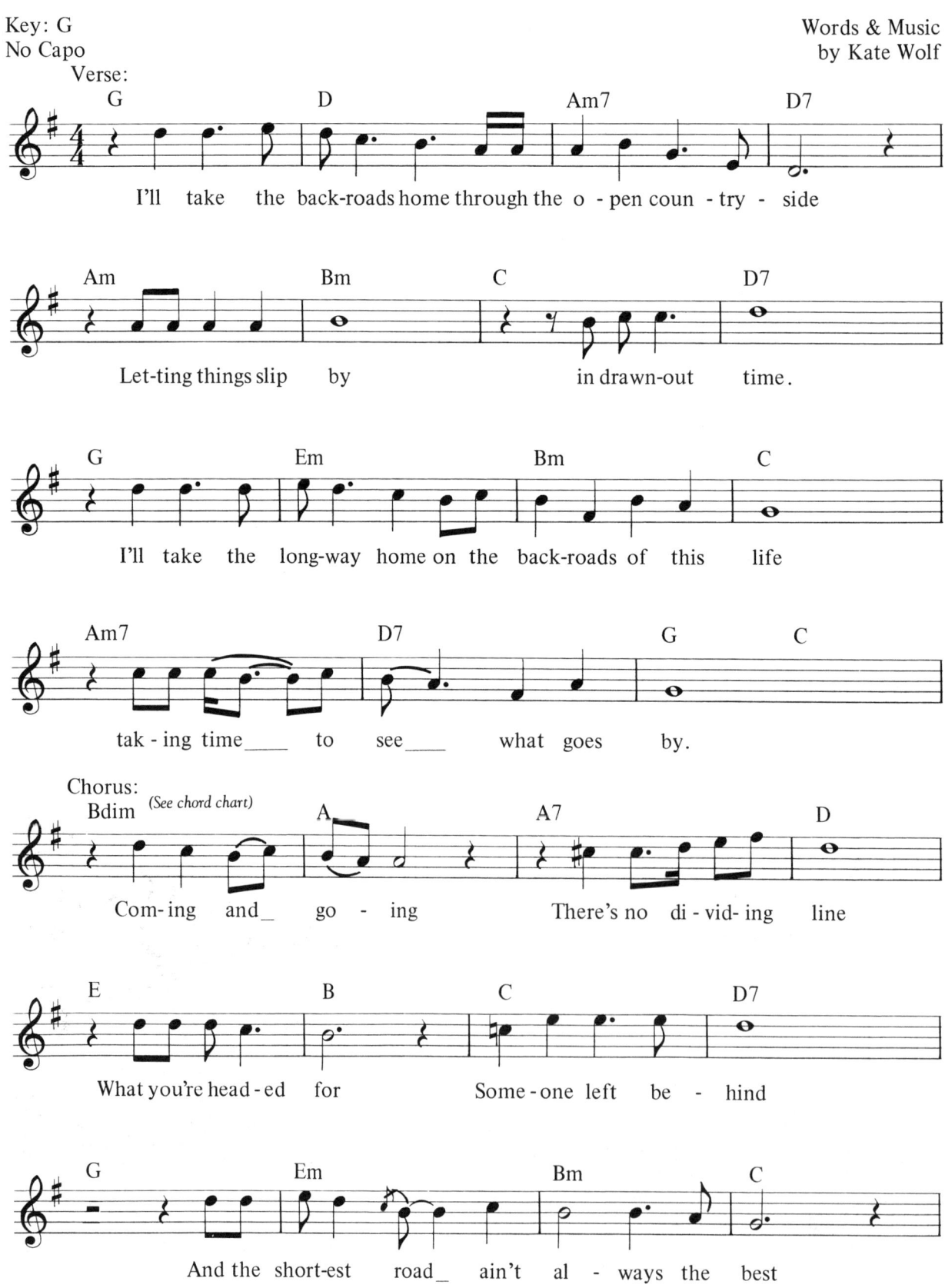

Some-time____ let a back-road take you home

I'll take the backroads home through the open countryside
Letting things slip by in drawn out time
I'll take the long way home on the backroads of this life
Taking time to see what goes by

  Chorus: Coming and going, there's no dividing line
           What you're headed for, someone left behind
           And the shortest road ain't always the best
           Sometime let a back road take you home

A back road is so easy, it just rambles on and on
Take it or leave it as it rolls along
Drifts through things it cannot change, and doesn't even try
Wouldn't that be something for you and I

  Chorus:

Anyplace you're bound, you'll get there someday
You're the one who chooses what to see along the way
And when the heartaches seem too much for you to bear
There's a back road winding everywhere.

  Chorus:

Sonoma County back roads

Don Coffin and Kate at Stern Grove, San Francisco

2

LINES ON THE PAPER

I Don't Know Why

Key: G
No Capo

Words & Music
by Kate Wolf

You're not the sweet-est man that I_____ ev-er knew

And I don't pre-tend to un-der-stand_____ ev-ery-thing you do

And there've been nights I've lain a-wake_ with-out you

Also Tag:
I don't know why I should love you_____ But I_____ do

You're

22

You're not the sweetest one that I ever knew
And I don't pretend to understand everything you do.
There've been nights I've lain awake — without you
And I don't know why I should love you,
But I do.

You're not the kind words come easy to.
Sometimes you turn away and it's hard to be with you
And I get confused and wonder what to do
And I don't know why I should love you
But I do.

Well, you'll always have a heart that's partly wild
And I've seen you be as foolish as a baby child
And you've got that crazy, stubborn strength in you
And I don't know why I should love you
But I do.

Lines On The Paper

Key: C
No Capo

Words & Music
by Kate Wolf

24

Say   I'm   some - one   that   you've   known?

In an outdoor cafe you drew my picture, drinking coffee all alone
I looked up and I caught you staring, at a picture all your own.

       Tell me, what are you seeing?
       Do you think that I'm alone?
       And do those lines upon your paper
       Say I'm someone that you've known

Well I wonder what you'd do if I told you
That I'm a painter just like you
I paint your picture with these words
Instead of brushes like you do

Now it's a writer or a painter, who can take a stranger home,
Captured in the lines upon the paper in a picture or a poem.

       Do you see what I'm seeing
       That you're another one alone.
       And do these lines upon my paper
       Say you're someone that I've known?

You're Not Standing Like You Used To

Key: Fm
Capo: 1st fret
Verse:

Words & Music
by Kate Wolf

I wish I could tell___ you how I feel to - night

It's been so long___ since I've seen you

You have-n't said____ but I can see so plain

Some-thing's been on your mind a - gain

Chorus:

'Cause you're not stand-ing like you used to

Your clothes are fit - ting you loos - er____ and

There's a tired shad - ow____ hid - ing in your eyes

You're look-ing like you could use a friend.

I wish I could tell you how I feel tonight
It's been so long since I've seen you
You haven't said, but I can see so plain
Something's been on your mind again

Chorus: Cause, you're not standing like you used to
Your clothes are fitting you looser
There's a tired shadow hiding in your eyes
And you're looking like you could use a friend

And I wish I could make you happy some way
But that would be a lie and you know it.
Find what you really care about
Then live a life that shows it

Cause, you're not standing like you used to
Your clothes are fitting you looser
There's a tired shadow hiding in your eyes
And you're looking like you could use a friend.

I wish I could say that I thought things would change
You've had so many try to love you
Too many years thinking you could see it all
Until a woman saw right through you

You're not standing like you used to
Your clothes are fitting you looser
There's a tired shadow hiding in your eyes
And you're looking like you could use a friend.

Picture Puzzle

Key: A
No Capo

Words & Music
by Kate Wolf

Verse:

I'm pick-ing up__ the piec - es   trying to fit the holes in this

pic - ture puz - zle   you left me long a - go   The

hard - est puz - zle   that I can see,   just a

pile of lit - tle piec - es   that makes no sense to me.

Chorus:

'Cause we were to - geth - er   now we're a -

part pick-ing up the piec - es of my____ heart   I

thought my heart would mend,__ and   babe, you know I've tried,   But the

pic - ture on the cov - er does - n't match the one in - side.

I'm picking up the pieces, trying to fit the holes
In this picture puzzle you left me long ago
The hardest puzzle that I can see
Just a pile of little pieces that makes no sense to me.
    Cause we were together, now we're apart
    And I'm picking up the pieces of my heart.
I thought my heart would mend, and babe, you know I've tried
But the picture on the cover doesn't match the one inside.

I'm holding the pieces, not knowing where to start
With this jigsaw puzzle you've made of my heart
A pretty picture puzzle should fit so easily
But the picture that you left me doesn't match the one I see
    Cause we were together, now we're apart
    And I'm picking up the pieces of my heart
The puzzle looked so easy 'til we tried to play the game
The pieces fit together, but the picture's not the same.

From left: Rick Byars, Blair Hardman, Kate, Paul Ellis, Don Coffin and Eddie B. Barlow (The Wildwood Flower 1977)

29

The Heart

Words & Music
by Kate Wolf

Key: Em
No Capo

Verse:

There is a heart locked in a box of pain

Want-ing so long to be free

And want-ing more to be in love a-gain___ Not be-

liev-ing an-y-one can turn the key

Chorus I :

There is a sto-ry that's been told be-fore

Of a good love_ that went bad

And of one who gave so much he gave him-self a-way And

left the heart so emp - ty and so sad

Chorus II :

Here is the strong-est heart that an - y - one __ has known

Locked up so long and go - ing blind

And in its dark - ness it does not see

It could break out an - y time

Tag:

It could break out an - y time

Song Structure:

First Verse
Chorus I
Second Verse
Chorus II
Third Verse
Chorus II

(Repeat to 2nd Verse before Chorus)

There is a heart locked in a box of pain
Wanting so long to be free
And wanting more to be in love again
Not believing anyone can turn the key.
> There is a story that's been told before
> Of a good love that went bad
> And of one who gave so much he gave himself away
> And left the heart so empty and so sad.

Friends who come to feed the heart
Are turned away by the walls within
The heart grows more lonely in its box of pain
It gives love but it cannot take it in.
> Here is the strongest heart that anyone has known
> Locked up so long and going blind
> And in its darkness it does not see
> It could break out anytime.

There is something that always seems so clear
From the outside looking in
When the heart is empty and it cannot feel
Let someone fill it once again.
> Here is the strongest heart that anyone has known
> Locked up so long and going blind
> And in its darkness it does not see
> It could break out anytime.

Cyrus Clarke, Kate, Bill Griffin

The Trumpet Vine

Key: B
Capo: 2nd fret

Words & Music
by Kate Wolf

The trum-pet vine grew in the kitch-en win-dow And

bloomed bright or-ange on the wall

You sat in the morn-ing light hold-ing a gui-tar_____ As the

first sum-mer rain be-gan to fall

Like the gen-tle rain-drops your words fell in the air

Mak-ing things so clear as we qui-et-ly sat there

It re-mind-ed me of oth-er times You had come be-

fore   And brought a   song   or   just walked in   through the kitch-en   door.

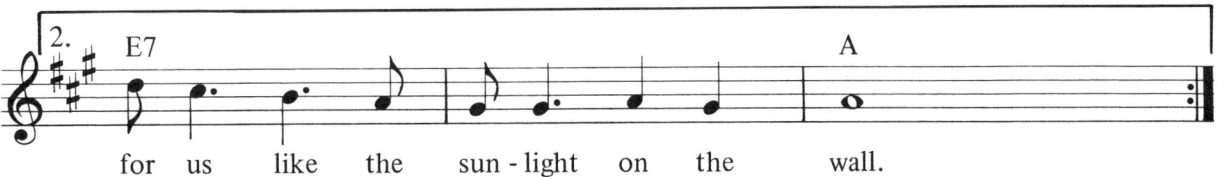

for   us   like   the   sun - light   on   the   wall.

walk - ing   through   the   kitch - en   door.

The trumpet vine grew in the kitchen window
And bloomed bright orange on the wall
You sat in the morning light, holding a guitar
As the first summer rain began to fall

> Like the gentle raindrops
> Your words fell in the air
> Making things so clear
> As we quietly sat there

It reminded me of other times you had come before
And brought a song or just walked in through the kitchen door.

Now it seems the truest words I ever heard from you
Were said at kitchen tables we have known
'Cause somehow in that warm room, with coffee on the stove,
Our hearts were really most at home.

> Sitting at a table
> Looking hard at you
> Catching up on stories
> Of the things we'd tried to do

It seems we really said the most when we didn't talk at all
Let the songs speak for us like the sunlight on the wall.

Now as we come and go, in sunshine and in rain,
Some years are seen more clearly than the rest
And if it weren't for kitchen songs and mornings spent with friends
We all might lose the things we love the best

> I can see you sitting there
> Beneath the trumpet vine
> The sunlight through the window
> In the kitchen in my mind

You came when you were needed, I could not ask for more
Than to turn to find you walking through the kitchen door.

I Never Knew My Father

Key: C
No Capo

Sung one octave higher

Words & Music
by Kate Wolf

Verse:

It was twen-ty five years a - go when I be-gan my life The

sec - ond child of a wom-an who tried hard to raise us right. She

mar - ried a man when I was just a babe Who

treat-ed me just like_ his own, ev - en giv-ing me his name

Chorus:

I nev - er knew my_ fa - ther, I on - ly knew his name.

(I) nev - er knew the way he___ moved, how he talked or what he said.__

Now I'm grown and my mom-ma says, "You're like your Dad - dy just__ the same."

36

It was twenty-five years ago
When I began my life
The second child of a woman
Who tried hard to raise us right.
She married a man, when I was just a babe
Who treated me just like his own,
Even giving me his name.

    I never knew my father, I only knew his name
    I never knew the way he moved
    How he talked, or what he said
    Now I'm grown and mama says
    "You're like your daddy, just the same"

Sometimes I got to wondering
About this man I never knew
When I'd find myself into something
Just the way he used to do
Heard stories all my life
Of how he loved to sing
And how he would take apart
And fix most anything.

    Chorus:

Now I can't say that I don't care
That he died before I was born
I get to asking why he did
And I'll probably ask some more.
My life's been good,
I can't say that I've had it bad
But now I'm seeing years
that my dad never had.

    Chorus:

Amazed To Find

Key: A
No Capo

Words & Music
by Kate Wolf

mazed   to   find   that   you're   still   on   my____   mind

After all is said and done
A few things lost, a few things won,
I can say I've had a full and a happy life.
But in the quiet of the night
When I turn out the light
I'm amazed to find that you're still on my mind.

    I'm amazed to find, I'm amazed to find
    that you're still on my mind

'Cause it will hit me without warning
Sometimes early in the morning
I'm amazed to find that you're still on my mind.

I could be talking with my friends
Or out walking when day ends
Or just doing all the things that fill my time.
But at the closing of the day
When my troubles fade away
I'm amazed to find that you're still on my mind.

    I'm amazed to find, I'm amazed to find
    That you're still on my mind

'Cause it will hit me without warning
Sometimes early in the morning
I'm amazed to find that you're still on my mind.

From Left: Che Greenwood, Al McKinney, Kate, Bruce Utah Phillips, Faith Petric, Fred Holstein, Tom Scribner, Dave Van Ronk and J.B. Freeman
   In front: Bodie Wagner.

Everybody's Looking For The Same Thing

Key: G
No Capo
Verse:

Words & Music
by Kate Wolf
and Hugh Shacklett

40

Three bed - rooms, ab - so - lute - ly   free.

Outside a country store there's a board on the wall
That's filled with cards of every size.
And what the folks are looking for is written there to see.
Reading it, it comes as no surprise

> That everybody's looking for the same thing
> The same thing, it's plain to see
> It's an old Chevy, a bass player
> A country house on three acres,
> Three bedrooms, absolutely free.

There's someone going to Boston with a guitar and a dog
And a lady with a goat to give away.
There's ten free kittens, a square dance on Sunday,
And Cindy, please get in touch with Ray.

> Chorus:

Know your future, it's in the stars — fifteen dollars or fix my car
You can call mornings or evenings until nine.
Do you want to lose weight, meditate? Herbal remedies you can take
and massages given at your house or mine.

> Chorus:

So if you're needing something and you don't know where to start
Just make yourself a card that says it all.
Use the words that say it best, include a number and address
And pin it up with the others on the wall.

> Chorus:

Kate and Hugh Shacklett

The Lilac And The Apple

Written in A
Unaccompanied Vocal

Words & Music
by Kate Wolf

A li - lac__ bush and an ap - ple tree Were stand-ing in the woods

Out on the hill a - bove the_ town, Where once a farm - house stood

In the win - ter the leaves are___ bare And no one sees the_ signs Of a

house that stood and a gar - den that grew, And life in an - oth - er time.

A Lilac bush and an Apple tree
Were standing in the woods
Out on the hill above the town,
Where once a farmhouse stood.
In the winter the leaves are bare
And no one sees the signs
Of a house that stood and a garden that grew
And life in another time.

One Spring when the buds came bursting forth
And grass grew on the land,
The Lilac spoke to the Apple tree
As only an old friend can.
Do you think, said the Lilac, this might be the year
When someone will build here once more?
Here by the cellar, still open and deep,
There's room for new walls and a floor.

Oh no, said the Apple, there are so few
Who come here on the mountain this way
And when they do, they don't often see
Why we're growing here, so far away.
A long time ago we were planted by hands
That worked in the mines and the mills
When the country was young and the people who came
Built their homes in the hills.

But now there are cities, the roads have come
And no one lives here today
And the only signs of the farms in the hills
Are the things not carried away.
Broken dishes, piles of boards,
A tin plate, an old leather shoe.
And an Apple tree still bending down
And a Lilac where a garden once grew.

Lay Me Down Easy

Key: G
No Capo

Words & Music
by Kate Wolf

Verse:

G   Em   C   D7

Sit - ting in the sun - shine, Trying to sing the blues a - way

G   C   D

Won-d'ring why they came And how long they'll stay

G   Em   C   D7

Pick-ing out a lit - tle tune I nev - er heard be - fore

Bm   C   D7

Yes and wish - ing you were here at the door

Chorus:

G   C   D7

Won't you lay me down eas - y

G   C   D7

Lay me down eas - y in my mind 'Cause

G   Em   C   D7

babe, I've got the blues___ And there's some-thing you can do

44

You can   lay   me   down   eas - y   in   my

mind   In   my   mind.

Sitting in the sunshine
Trying to sing the blues away
Wondering why they came
And how long they'll stay.
Picking out a little tune
I never heard before
Yes and wishing you were here
— at the door

> Won't you lay me down easy,
> Lay me down easy in my mind
> 'Cause babe, I've got the blues
> And there's something you can do.
> You can lay me down easy in my mind,
> In my mind.

Well babe, you know how it is
When you wake up feeling old.
You wonder if you're doing
What you should.
And everyone around you —
They can't read what's on your mind
And they might not want to
If they could.

> Chorus:

Now the seasons of my life
They go turning through the days.
I've seen bitter winters
Come and go.
And here I am in sunny times
Not feeling like I could
And wondering when the winds
Will start to blow.

> Chorus:

Bodega Bay landscape

Kate and Bill Griffin at Arch Studios, Berkeley

3

SAFE
AT
ANCHOR

Safe At Anchor

Key: A
No Capo

Words & Music
by Kate Wolf

Verse:

A   **B7**   **E**   **D**

Here I stand a - lone_ a - gain   reach-in' out a - cross_ the room

C#m   **D**   **A**   **B7**   **E**

Qui - et - ly the sun's_ gone down   and sail-ors seek the har - bor.

A   **B7**   **E7**   **D**

Look at us sail - in' in,_   decks a-wash but still a - float_

C#m   **D**   **A**   **E7**   **A**

And now the wind's come up_ to rock us on_ the wa - ter

Chorus:

C#m   **D**   **A**

Rid-ing out_ the storm, like a ship safe at an - chor

C#m   **D**   **E7**   **A**

Wait -in' out the long voy-age 'round the Cape of Hope we'll take her

48

Here I stand alone again,
 reaching out across the room
Quietly the sun's gone down
 and sailors seek the harbor.
Look at us sailing in,
 decks awash, but still afloat
And now the wind's come up
 to rock us on the water.

Chorus

 Riding out the storm
 like a ship safe at anchor.
 Waiting out the long voyage,
 'round the Cape of Hope we'll take her.

In the calm before the storm
 sunny days and smoother waters.

When we hit the seventh wave,
 we found a line and caught her
Look into my eyes,
 let me see where you've been sailing.
Like you I've felt the storm
 and heard the wild waves wailing.

Chorus

Steer clear of the shore,
 the coast is rough and rocky
It's the deepest channel that runs most true,
 the brightest stars that mark her.
Steady as she goes,
 there's no turning back the sailors
With the ship on course and the sea wind fair,
 there's no need to fail her.

Chorus

Kate and Nina Gerber

Early Morning Melody

Key: F
Capo: 1st fret

Words & Music
by Kate Wolf

(An) Ear-ly morn-ing mel - o - dy__ play-ing in the scen-er - y of

my mind   Rain-y days and o - cean tides,__

through the hills and green-wood sides Like a wind - chime

I think of you that way a lot,__ sing-ing to the cof-fee pot and the

kitch-en wall   Al-ways up be - fore the sun_

pick-ing out some pret-ty run, on the strings Like a wa - ter -

fall   like a wa - ter - fall_____

An early morning melody
      playing in the scenery of my mind.
Rainy days and ocean tides,
      through the hills and greenwood sides
Like a windchime.

I think of you that way a lot,
      singing to the coffeepot and the kitchen wall.
Always up before the sun,
      picking out some pretty run, on the strings
Like a waterfall, like a waterfall . . .

You've given me so many songs,
      ones that kept me going on when I'd wonder why.
Weaving through the busy days,
      they were colors in the misty haze,
Like rainbow rhymes.

Reminding me that even prison walls
      turn to dust and fall before the open sky.
And love can find you in the darkest hour,
      touch you lightly as a flower on colored wings,
Like a butterfly, like a butterfly . . .

Thought I'd let you know
      I heard you singing soft and low when I woke today
I got up to play along,
      found myself with a morning song
To send your way.

Thanking you for all the times
      you've listened to these sunrise lines I've made for you.
I see your face before me now,
      smiling as if you know somehow, you've touched my day
Like the morning dew, like the morning dew . . .

Kate at KVRE Santa Rosa 1977

Sweet Love

Key: G
No Capo

Words & Music
by Kate Wolf

Sweet love, don't de - ny me just a hand to hold_

I may not al - ways be the one_ who sees

(I) Find my - self blind - ed from time to time_

Reach-ing out for some-one who can take the lead_

And in my wea - ri - ness I've tried to cry Al -

though my eyes_ are dry, I've cried in - side._____

Sweet love, don't deny me just a hand to hold;
    I may not always be the one who sees.
I find myself blinded from time to time,
    reaching out for someone who can take the lead.
And in my weariness I've tried to cry.
    Although my eyes are dry, I've cried inside.

Sweet love, let me lay myself beside you
    and listen to your breathing 'til it slows,
Long enough to dream a vision of my life
    wrapped up in the gentle wind that blows.
A vision of a life lived long ago —
    I see it, though the lights are low.

Sweet love, like the leaves that fall,
    the scenes go drifting by my eyes.
And I remember holding you,
    telling you that it would be alright.
You know the road looked straight ahead from far away.
    But it turned into a blind curve,
    And I've lost my way today.

She Rises Like The Dolphin

Key: F
Capo: 5th fret

Words & Music
by Kate Wolf

She ris - es like_ the dol - phin with the sea wind in her eyes. And the

sun - light cast - ing shad - ows___ like a paint - er's pal - ette knife.___

Her hair fans out a - round her, float - ing like_ a crown,__

She plays on the wa - ter and lets it pull_ her down___

Some - times she swims in the moon - light with the stars high a -

bove, The night sounds of the wa - ter speak - in' soft of

love, Her skin turns to vel - vet as she

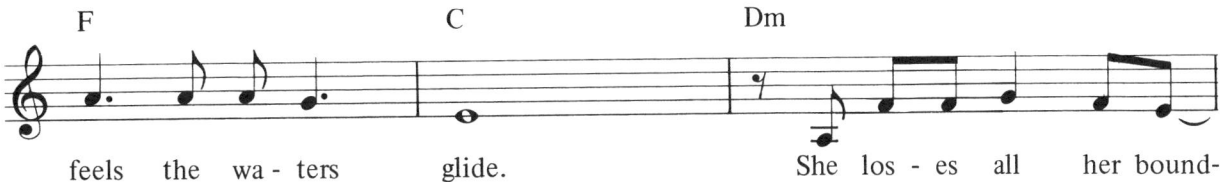

feels the wa - ters glide. She los - es all her bound-

'ries on this mag - ic car - pet ride._____

She rises like the dolphin
    with the sea wind in her eyes
And the sunlight casting shadows
    like a painter's palette knife.
Her hair fans out around her,
    floating like a crown.
She plays on the water
    and lets it pull her down.

    Sometimes she swims in moonlight
        with the stars high above
    And the nightsounds of the water
        speaking soft of love.
    Her skin turns to velvet
        as she feels the waters glide.
    She loses all her boundaries
        on this magic carpet ride.

You see ripples on the water
    and watch the shadows dance.
Then she's diving down
    and you're looking through a glass.
Like a one-way mirror
    her reflection's far below.
And where she was, she isn't now;
    that's all you really know.

Two swimmers in the water
    one of silver, one of gold
One below the surface,
    one reaching for a hold
One floating freely,
    one trying not to drown
A dreamer with two faces,
    a dolphin and a clown.

If you think you'll hold her
    in a shallow pool
Or catch her in a water fall,
    you're thinking like a fool.
She'll strike for the horizon
    like a ship out to sea
Leaving just illusions
    that look like memories.

    She wears the water like a mask,
        a brand new suit of clothes
    A player on the stage,
        an actress no one knows.
    See her roll and tumble,
        falling like a clown —
    A swimmer in the water
        that runs from higher ground.

Great Love Of My Life

Key: G
No Capo

Words & Music
by Kate Wolf

Great love of my life,_____ how I

feel you here be - side me, Watch-ing the clouds, turn

red at the close of day.____ And you know I think a - bout you

as the sun goes down And you're far a - way.

1,2,3,4,5. 6.

we paid the price

And we paid the price._____

Great love of my life, how I feel you here beside me
Watching the clouds turn red at the close of day.
And you know I think about you as the sun goes down
And you're far away.

Great love of my life, I see your face before me
As the day goes fading into night.
And it's all that I can do not to want you here beside me
In the firelight.

Great love of my life, you know it isn't easy
Saying goodbye to the good times that we knew.
But the hard times came and took us where we never
        thought we'd go,
And left us broken, me and you.

Great love of my life, the flames are leaping higher
Talking to me in the quiet, empty room
So happy and so sad with the twisted pain of love
That left too soon.

Remember the time we stood laughing like small children
Caught in the rain and they took our photograph
With our arms around each other and our eyes on fire
Looking out at the rain running off our hats.

Great love of my life, the first time that we touched
We were so hungry it took us by surprise
And it never changed all the years we were as one.
We tasted it all; we paid the price
And we paid the price.

Kate and Bill Griffin

Shining!

Key: B
Capo: 2nd fret

Words & Music
by Kate Wolf

Verse:

Oh, love, it's your blue eyes___ turn-ing to black

Shin-ing down on me___ as I lie here on my back, And that

love - light shines deep - er than ev - en I can see; It

makes my heart glad it's shin-ing down on me._____

Chorus:

Shin-ing in the morn - ing shin-ing in the eve - ning_____

____ Shin-ing in the sum-mer_ and the win-ter too

Makes me sing with a glad_____ heart sing - in my sor - row,

58

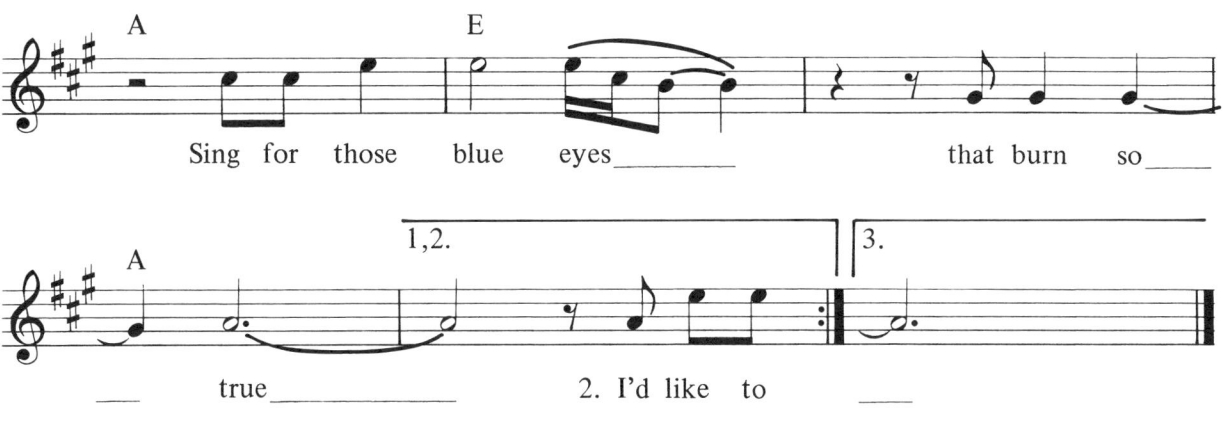

Sing for those blue eyes_____ that burn so_____

1,2. | 3.

_____ true_____ 2. I'd like to _____

Oh love, it's your blue eyes
    turning to black
Shining down on me
    as I lie here on my back
And that lovelight shines deeper
    than even I can see
It makes my heart glad
    it's shining down on me.

    Chorus

    Shining in the morning,
    Shining in the evening
    Shining in the summer
    and the winter too.
    Makes me sing with a glad heart
    Sing in my sorrow,
    Sing for those blue eyes
    That burn so true.

I'd like to wrap you in my blankets,
    yes, and ride that morning train.
Lie warm and soft beside you,
    listening to the rain
Rolling down the valley
    on its journey in the wind
And watch that light of love
    come shining down again.

    Chorus:

You get that look in your eyes, love
    it's something I can't name
I've seen that look before
    just not on something tame.
It's a little lost and lonely,
    a spirit burning free,
That makes my heart glad
    it's shining down on me.

    Chorus:

September Song

Key: F
Capo: 3rd fret

Words & Music
by Kate Wolf

Verse:

The wild geese flew o - ver - head in Penn - syl - van - ia I

thought of a few_ choice words I ought to send you. And you

know if I thought it was right I'd pre - tend you were here___ with me to -

night The ghost of a fron - tier la - dy walked through the

tall rooms. Of an old On - tar - i - o farm - house un - der a

full moon And we sat in the kitch-en all night,

Drink-ing good whis - key un - til the morn-ing light. Did you

Chorus:

ev - er think I would go Out on this road___ you told me I___ would

take so long a - go?_____

The wild geese flew overhead in Pennsylvania
I thought of a few choice words I ought to send you
And you know if I thought it was right
I'd pretend that you were here with me tonight.

The ghost of a frontier lady walked through the tall rooms
Of an old Ontario farmhouse under a full moon
And we sat in the kitchen all night,
Drinking good whiskey until the morning light.

> Did you ever think I would go
> Out on this road you told me I would take
> So long ago?

On a Roanoke backroad, laughing beside a cold stove
We sang for old black Francis & Bessie, songs about true love.
All the songs I ever knew
Came back to me and brought me back to you.

The leaves were turning, we felt the summer passing
Knowing things were changing, even without asking.
Like a photograph faded in time
In a cabin lost in the Blue Ridge mountain pines.

> Did you ever think I would go
> Out on this road you told me I would take
> So long ago?

Now the wind is blowing cold across the bay
And Massachusetts seems so far away
From the California tides,
The rolling hills and roads I used to ride.

So I'm leaving in the morning, seeing faces
Of friends I leave behind in all these places
And though I'm coming home,
I'm not coming back to California all alone.

> Yes, you always knew I would go
> Out on this road you took yourself once,
> So long ago.

Seashore Mountain Lady

Key: F
Capo: 1st fret

Words & Music
by Kate Wolf

Verse:

Down be-side the o-cean, the door-ways face the sea Look-ing out a-cross the wa-ter on e-ter-ni-ty Down from the moun-tains like the roll-ing tides Comes the sea-shore moun-tain la-dy with the haunt-ed eyes___

Chorus:

Can you tell me just how you came to be Liv-ing in the moun-tains by the roll-ing sea? Did you leave be-hind a shel-ter for your

62

long hair blow-ing free? 'Cause that's what your eyes say to me.

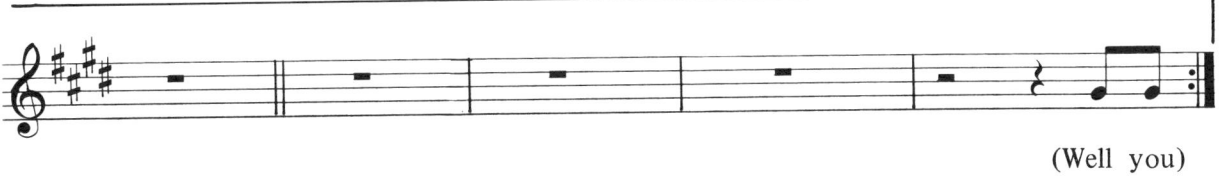

(Well you)

round her, her hair blow-in' free._____

Down beside the ocean the doorways face the sea
Looking out across the water on eternity
Down from the mountains, like the rolling tides
Comes the seashore mountain lady with the haunted eyes.

    Can you tell me just how you came to be
    Living in the mountains by the rolling sea?
    Did you leave behind a shelter for your long hair
        blowing free?
    'cause that's what your eyes say to me.

You sit there with your baby and you're all dressed in blue
Wearing roses on your shoulders and mud-caked shoes
And you're listening to the wind as it sings to you
From someplace down inside yourself as children often do.

Did you come here for the living that makes you
    try your wings?
For tasting cold and hunger and leaving pretty
    things?
Did you come here for someone who works with
    the land,
Who'll reach inside your soul with his hands?

Living in the mountains by the rolling sea,
You live with the wind always blowing free
That blows in the rain and bends the growing trees,
And tears at your heart like a seashore mountain lady.

    And she moves with the grace of the deer and the
        squirrel,
    High in the mountains on the edge of the world.
    With her haunted eyes turned toward the sea,
    Her skirts wrapped around her and her hair
        blowing free.

Looking Back At You

Key: F
Capo: 3rd fret
Verse:

Words & Music
by Kate Wolf

I nev-er wrote a song for you__ that touched me like you do_____

We're in this to - geth - er now,__ now we're fin - 'ly through

You al-ways want-ed it to feel that way and you gave it all__ your heart__

__ But I did - n't know my mind and it

kept us far a - part____ Now I see in your eyes

The love I al - ways knew_____ (But) for the

first time in a long time it's in me Look-in' back at you.__

64

I never wrote a song for you
        that touched me like you do
We're in this together now,
        now we're finally through.
You always wanted it to feel that way
        and you gave it all your heart.
But I didn't know my mind
        and it kept us far apart.

        Now I see in your eyes
        The love I always knew
        (But) for the first time in a long time,
        it's in me —
        Looking back at you.

When you let me go
        like I said I wanted to
The farther I went away
        the closer I felt to you.

Now we both sit here crying
        like we never could do before.
And the best part of it all
        is not lying to you anymore.

        Chorus:

Wipe away the tears;
        it's funny how love's done
Just when you let it go
        it comes back on the run.
And if I can give you anything
        to take along with you
It's all the love I found
        looking back at you.

        Chorus:

Kate and Nina Gerber at the No Nukes Rally, San Francisco Civic Center 1979

Two-Way Waltz

Key: A
No Capo

Words & Music
by Kate Wolf

Verse:

You're a quick-sil - ver la - dy, A child__ of the morn - ing, A
flow - er by day,__ A slow fire by__ night. But
he's taught you things, For all that you've shown him. He's a
gaz - er of stars,__ A blue crys-tal light.__ And

Chorus:

some-times__ he cries And he says things____ That
pierce you To your soul But
he's still a man Who loves you

66

And it hurts To let you__ go.

You're a quicksilver lady,
    A child of the morning
A flower by day,
    A slow fire by night.
But he's taught you things,
    For all that you've shown him.
He's a gazer of stars,
    A blue crystal light.

And sometimes he cries
    And he says things
That pierce you
    To your soul
But he's still a man
    Who loves you
And it hurts
    To let you go.

You're a man with the power
    Of rattlesnake lightening,
Hard like the mountains
    But soft like the sun.
And she's taught you things
    For all that you've shown her
She's a weaver of visions
    In threads finely spun.

And sometimes she cries
    And she walks away
Held by the dreams
    That find her.
But she's still a woman
    Who loves you
And her heart
    Will always remind her.

So dance for the day
    But watch for the signs
That point out your way
    When the doubt fills your eyes.
And try to believe
    That the sweetest hello
Always comes after
    The hardest goodbye.

For two ways can sometimes
    Make one
That's stronger
    Than either alone.
So dancers join hands
    For the two-way waltz
But take the steps
    On your own.

Nina Gerber and Kate

CLOSE
TO
YOU

Across The Great Divide

Key: A
No Capo

Words & Music
by Kate Wolf

Verse:

I've been walk - ing_____ in my sleep count - ing

trou - bles_____ 'stead of count - ing sheep. Where the

years went I can't say I just

turned a - round and they've gone a - way.____ But I've been

Chorus:

(It's) Gone a - way____ in yes - ter - day____

and I find___ my - self on____ the moun - tain - side

Where the riv - ers change di - rec - tion A - cross the great di - vide.___

I've been walking in my sleep
counting troubles, 'stead of counting sheep.
Where the years went, I can't say;
I just turned around and they've gone away.

     Gone away — in yesterday,
     and I find myself on the mountainside,
     Where the rivers change direction
     Across the Great Divide.

I've been sifting through the layers
of dusty books and faded papers.
They tell a story I used to know;
one that happened so long ago.

     Chorus:

Well I heard the owl calling
softly as the night was falling.
With a question, and I replied
but he's gone across the borderline.

     Chrous:

 The finest hour, that I have seen,
is the one that comes between
the edge of night and the break of day,
When the darkness rolls away.

     Chorus:

The Great Divide in the Canadian Rockies.

Leggett Serenade

Key: A
Capo: 2nd fret
Verse:

Words & Music
by Kate Wolf

Chop-ping wood in the rain,__ the axe swings up_ and falls a - gain;__

I watch you move so smooth-ly___ in the dance.

Lis-tening to the hol-low sound of split-ting logs_ as they hit the ground,__

I'd build a fire_ for you if I had the chance.__ Let the

chips fall__ where_ they can.___ I've tried my_ best to un-der-stand Why we

stand out here in the rain___ in our an - ger and_ our pain____

A-fraid to feel_ the love that's in our hands.___

72

Chopping wood in the rain,
the axe swings up and falls again;
I watch you move so smoothly
in the dance.
Listening to the hollow sound
of splitting logs as they hit the ground,
I'd build a fire for you
if I had the chance.

  Let the chips fall where they can
  I've tried my best to understand.
  Why we stand out here in the rain
  in our anger and our pain,
  Afraid to feel the love
  that's in our hands.

Love that was so strong
stopped you short when it came along,
Sometimes I wonder why
you ever stayed.

'Cause when you turn away
and save yourself for a rainy day,
Love grows weak and then
it starts to fade.

  Chorus:

In the winter's wet and cold
some people change and some just grow old;
The years go by
in spite of what you do.
I'd like to lay you down
and turn your twisted head around.
But babe, there's really nothing
that I can do.

  Chorus:

Wavy Gravy and Kate at the SEVA Benefit

Like A River

Key: G
No Capo

Words & Music
by Kate Wolf

Verse:

G

It's high on a moun-tain the warm winds are blow-in'_ (and) Where the winds are

Am   C   G

blow-in' to_____ there ain't no way of know-in'.___

Em   C   G

The moun-tain grass is short; it's dry and close to burn-in',____

Am   C   G

Cry-in' out for wa-ter as the sea-son's turn-ing.__

Chorus: Em   C   G

The sweet smell of the pines_____ the tall west-ern___ ce-dar__

Am   C   G

Drift-in' on the wind through the moun-tains Like a Riv-er._____

74

It's high on a mountain
the warm winds are blowing,
And where the winds are blowing to
there ain't no way of knowing.

The mountain grass is short;
it's dry and close to burning,
Crying out for water
as the season's turning.

The sweet smell of the pines,
the tall western cedar
Drifting on the wind
Through the mountains
Like a River.

I've been too long away
from this wild open sky
On the concrete trails that wind
through the canyons dark and wide.

With the sounds of people talking
in words of blue and grey,
Smells of doors and windows
closed against the day.

Chorus:

Now the dust lies thick and heavy
where my feet are falling
There's nothing but the sound
of the jaybirds calling.
My mind grows dry and thirsty
as the memories linger
Drifting on the wind
through the mountains
Like a River.

Chorus:

Kate and Nina Gerber at Sam's

Unfinished Life

Key: Dm
Capo: 5th fret
Verse:

Words & Music
by Kate Wolf

It's an un-fin-ished life that I find lies be-fore me: An

o-pen-end-ed dream, and I don't want to wake I've crossed so man-y riv-ers__ in

search of crystal foun-tains. I've found the tru-est paths al-ways lead thru'mountains I've seen

wa-ter on the sky__ and fire burn-ing on the lake.____

Chorus:

You said to me,_ "I can-not make you hap-py Like a wound-ed bird, you must

find the strength to fly. Time can paint the tree-tops with col-ors of the rainbow But you

can-not find the end_ no mat-ter how you try."____

76

It's an unfinished life
that I find lies before me;
an open-ended dream
and I don't want to wake.
I've crossed so many rivers
in search of crystal fountains;
I've found the truest paths
always lead through mountains.
I've seen water on the sky,
and fire burning on the lake.

    You said to me
    "I cannot make you happy
    Like a wounded bird,
    you must find the strength to fly.
    Time can paint the treetops
    with colors of the rainbow
    But you cannot find the end,
    no matter how you try."

It's a journey with my soul
that I am taking.
One that only goes
from the cradle to the grave.

Going 'round in circles
like painted dancing horses,
Up and down we ride
on the wooden courses.
And light from a lover's eyes
is all that I can save.

    Chorus:

So I'll take the day and run
out across the open fields,
Where the grass grows high
and the shadows fall.
Where my eyes can see
all the colors in the air.
So quiet that the wind
whistles in my hair
And takes the rising dust
and carries it away.

    Chorus:

Friend Of Mine

Key: G
Capo: 5th fret
Tune low E string to D

Words by Kate Wolf
Music by Kate Wolf,
Nina Gerber and Ford James

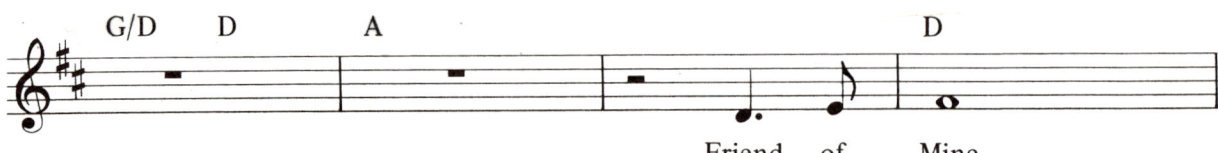

Friend of Mine

I can't un-do__ the wrong.___ I could have

giv-en so much more___ than just these cra-zy songs._ I

walked down by the riv-er and I thought of you to-day;____ You

al-ways seemed to un-der-stand the words I couldn't say._____

But when we'd sing to-geth-er_____ those coun-try har-mo-nies___ I

nev - er heard a sweet - er voice come so eas - y

and so_____ free.

Friend of Mine___

Friend of Mine

___ free.

Friend of Mine
I can't undo the wrong.
I could have given so much more
than just these crazy songs.
I walked down by the river
and I thought of you today;
You always seemed to understand
the words I couldn't say.

But when we'd sing together
those country harmonies,
I never heard a sweeter voice
come so easy and so free.

Friend of Mine
at times you were so wise,
with the sweet ways of a playful child
and sorrow in your eyes.
You came riding through
but your heart made you stay.
I could use some of your honesty
now that you've gone away.

I can feel your footsteps
walking here with me.
I never heard a sweeter voice
come so easy and so free.

Friend of Mine
singing to me now,
I wanted to say I cared;
I didn't quite know how.
Now driving on these dusty roads
where we spent so many days,
Your songs wrap close around me
like the heavy summer haze.

The coast of California
holds me like your melodies.
I never heard a sweeter voice
come so easy and so free.

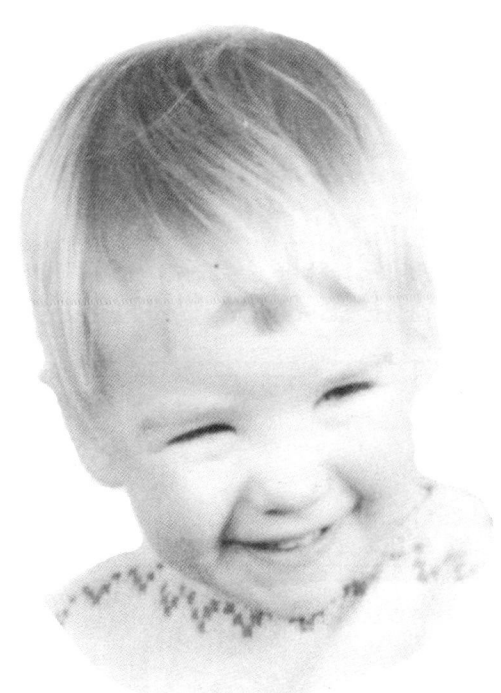

Love Still Remains

Key: B♭
Capo: 3rd fret

Words & Music
by Kate Wolf

Verses 1 & 2:

I went home to a place I swore I'd nev - er see__ a - gain.

Lord, it's dif-ferent now;___ there's hard-ly an - y - thing__that has-n't changed.

2nd verse only

___ And the friends I've known 1. have grown and moved a-
2. I moved a-way and changed my

way. But the love I felt for_ you___ still re - mains.___
name

Chorus:

It re - mains,_____ it blows down the

dust - y streets and rides the fal - ling rain.____ And

rolls___ like a tum-ble - weed out on the o - pen range__ The

love I felt_ for_ you___ still re - mains._   I walked

I went home
to a place I swore I'd never see again.
Lord, it's different now;
there's hardly anything that hasn't changed.
And the friends I've known
have grown and moved away.
But the love I felt for you
still remains.

    It remains,
    it blows down the dusty streets
    And rides the falling rain.
    And rolls like a tumbleweed
    out on the open range.
    The love I felt for you
    still remains.

I walked down
past the buildings standing empty and unused.
Where you asked me one more time
if I'd stay, and then you cried when I refused.

That was long ago;
I moved away and I changed my name.
But the love I felt for you
still remains.

    Chorus:

I could say
that I always thought you'd be there when I came
But you wanted more
and I could say the same.
Now I'm leaving
like the whistle on a lonesome boxcar train.
But the love I felt for you
still remains.

    Chorus:

Kate and Nina Gerber

Eyes Of A Painter

Key: B♭
Capo: 3rd fret
Verse:

Words & Music
by Kate Wolf

Grey - haired and flint - eyed, his sun - burned face lined,____

Grand - pa was a man__ of few__ words.

He had a way__ of not want - ing to say____ an - y more__

___ than he thought would be heard. The

long years of liv - in' day to day giv - in' had

carved out a map on his face. With

lit - tle to lose he'd learned how to choose and his

84

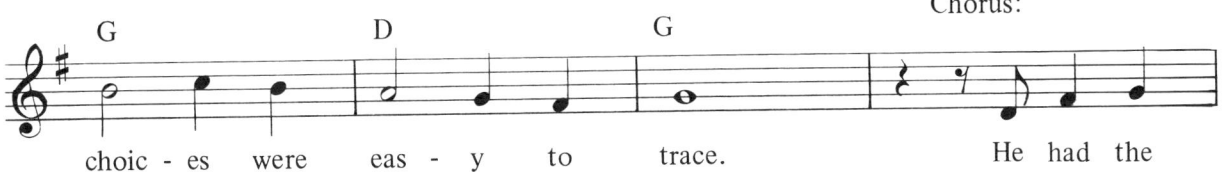

choic - es were eas - y to trace. *Chorus:* He had the

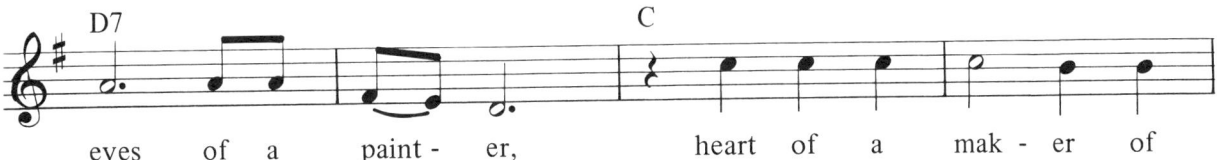

eyes of a paint - er, heart of a mak - er of

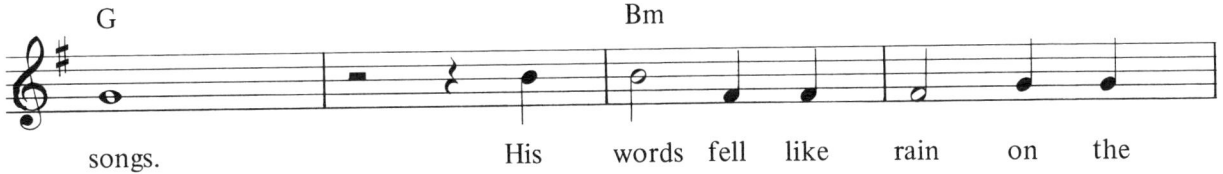

songs. His words fell like rain on the

dry des-ert plain, Pre-cious and so quick -ly gone.

Greyhaired and flint-eyed, his sunburned face lined
Grandpa was a man of few words.
But he had a way of not wanting to say
any more than he thought would be heard.

The long years of living and day to day giving
had carved out a map on his face.
With little to lose, he'd learned how to choose
and his choices were easy to trace.

> He had the eyes of a painter,
> the heart of a maker of songs
> His words fell like rain
> on the dry desert plain,
> Precious and so quickly gone.

From a long line of teachers and white Baptist preachers
He was born with an Indian will.
His quiet dark eyes reading the light
as he rode in the low Osage hills.

His school was the prairie, the Sage, the wild berry,
the Quail, the wide open sky,
The Cottonwood thicket by the slow rolling river,
the Redbud and the hot cattle drive.

Chorus:

There were days filled with thinking, nights with the
drinking for a lost love that raged like a storm.
But how his eyes smiled when he'd talk to a child,
the rough hands so gentle and warm.

His strong arms were brown where the long sleeves
rolled down on his faded blue cotton shirt.
When times got hard he'd go out in the yard
and cuss away some of his hurt.

Chorus:

Now the garden's grown dusty, the handaxe lies rusty,
the door's banging hard in the wind,
Grandpa's store is closed down, like most of the town,
and it won't be open again.

And the big white car sits out in the yard
of the house he built solid and true,
But I see his eyes burning tonight
like the stars in the sky he once knew.

Chorus:

Here In California

Key: G#
Capo: 1st fret

Words & Music
by Kate Wolf

Verse:

When I was young my ma-ma told me she said

"Child take your time. Don't

fall in love too quick-ly be-

fore you know your mind." She

held me 'round the shoul-ders (and) in a

voice so soft and kind She said

"Love can make you hap-py (and)

love_____ can rob____ you blind"____

Chorus:

Here_____ in Cal - i - for - nia   the

fruit hangs heav - y on the vine.____   And there's no

gold,   I thought I'd warn__ ya,   And the

hills turn brown in the sum-mer - time_____

When I was young my mama told me,
she said "Child take your time.
Don't fall in love too quickly,
before you know your mind."

She held me 'round the shoulders,
and in a voice so soft and kind
She said "Love can make you happy
and love can rob you blind."

    "Here in California
    the fruit hangs heavy on the vine.
    There's no gold
    I thought I'd warn ya
    And the hills turn brown
    in the summertime."

Now I may learn to love you
but I can't say when.
This morning we were strangers
and tonight we're only friends.

I'll take my time to know you;
I'll take my time to see.
There's nothing I won't show you
if you take your time with me.

    Chorus:

It's an old familiar story,
an old familiar rhyme.
To everything there is a season;
to every purpose there's a time.

A time to love and come together;
a time when love longs for a name,
A time for questions we can't answer,
'though we ask them just the same.

    Chorus:

Stone In The Water

Key: B
Capo: 2nd fret

Words & Music
by Kate Wolf

Verse:

Now babe, is that you cry - in' 'cause I'm not ly - in' next to you?

That sun go - ing down sure makes this lone - some town__ thir - ty shades of blue._____

Here in Min - ne - so - ta wait-ing out the sum-mer's hot - test night I think a - bout you walk - ing on__ the beach___ at home and I know you'll be__ al - right._____

Chorus:

Throw a stone in the wa - ter___ (and) Bless the son__ and daugh-ter of this

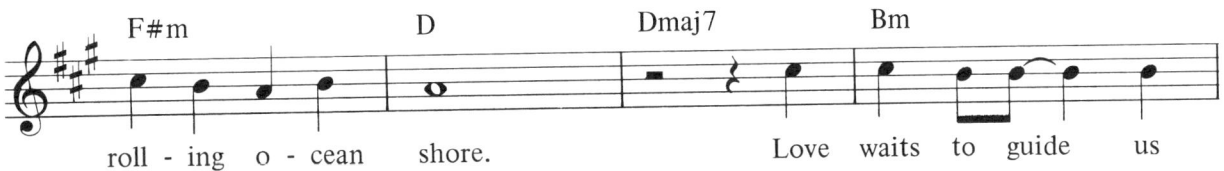

roll - ing o - cean shore. Love waits to guide us

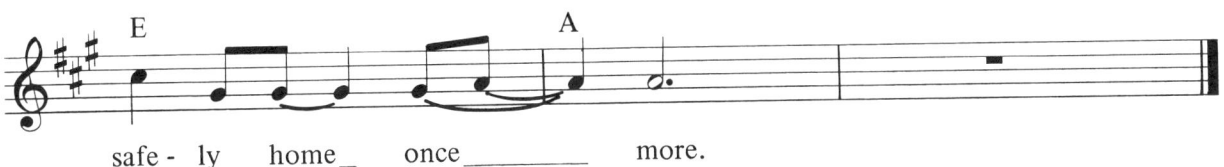

safe - ly home_ once_____ more.

Now babe, is that you crying
'cause I'm not lying next to you?
That sun going down
sure makes this lonesome town
Thirty shades of blue.

Here in Minnesota,
waiting out the summer's hottest night,
I think about you walking
on the beach at home
And I know you'll be alright.

    Throw a stone in the water;
    Bless the son and daughter
    of this rolling ocean shore.
    Love waits to guide us
    safely home once more.

You've been calling on the telephone,
spending all those hours alone 'cause you wanted to.
And writing letters everynight
it seemed right to say
Whatever came to you.

Now go down by the water
and make a wish for you and me.
And watch the shorebirds running in
as the tide
Goes running out to sea.

    Chorus:

Love is all around you
as the day falls fast asleep.
But all that I can send you now
is a love
That's only yours to keep.

People walking with their dogs,
stacking driftwood logs to make a fire.
As the sea pulls at the sun
the day flies on the run
Before the night's desire.

    Chorus:

Kate and Ford James

Close To You

Key: E
No Capo

Words & Music
by Kate Wolf

1. I like the way you smile, It re-minds me of a hap-py child,

It makes me feel a lit - tle less___ a - lone.

I miss you when you're gone,_____ The ho - urs___ they stretch on and on

Like wa - ter___ drip-ping slow - ly on a stone.

You're such a mys-ter - y,_____ The way you look at me_____ with that

light that shines from some-place I can't go._____ Did it

take you by__ sur - prise_____ when you re-al-ized

90

that you loved me, though you've nev-er told me so.

I like the way you smile
It reminds me of a happy child
It makes me feel a little less alone

I miss you when you're gone
The hours they stretch on and on
Like water dripping slowly on a stone

You're such a mystery,
The way you look at me
With that light that shines
from someplace I can't go.
Did it take you by surprise
when you realized
That you loved me — though
you've never told me so.

You know I want to say
So many things to you today
But you've got me feeling like I'm flying blind.

I think if you were here
The words would ring crystal clear
From this heart that's learning how to speak its mind.

You fight for truth with love
you're an iron hand in a velvet glove
It's the kind of strength
that makes a gentle man.
But I'm a child of the wind —
I've been blown away but I'm back again.
I just don't know if you really understand.

Sunlight moves across the floor
There's a soft breeze through the open door
A sleepy cat lying on the windowsill.

On this lazy afternoon
Like honey on a silver spoon
The memory of your smile is with me still.

Don't tell me that it's wrong
to say I love you with a song.
When the words won't come,
I've seen you do it too.
This road winds along;
one day we'll be gone
But I'll have this song to bring me close to you.

Nina Gerber and Kate

5

GIVE
YOURSELF
TO
LOVE

Give Yourself To Love

Key: B
Capo: 4th fret

Words & Music
by Kate Wolf

Verse

Kind friends all gath-ered round there's some-thing I would say That what brings us__ to-geth-er here____ has blessed us all__ to-day____

Love has_ made a cir-cle that holds us all in-side Where stran-gers are as fam-i-ly_____ and lone-li-ness can't__ __ hide

Chorus:

You must give your-self_ to love____ if love is what you're af - ter O-pen up your heart_ to_____ the tears and laugh - ter And give your-self__ to love____

94

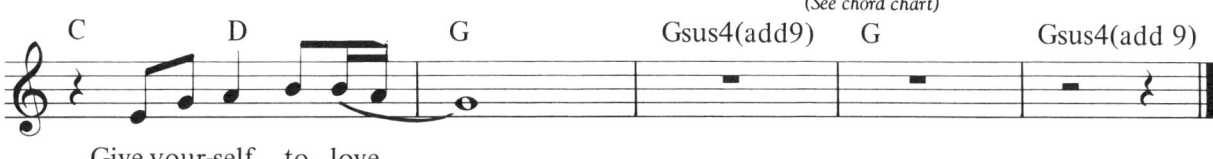

C   D   G   (See chord chart) Gsus4(add9)   G   Gsus4(add 9)

Give your-self   to   love_____

Kind friends all gathered 'round
there's something I would say
That what brings us together here
has blessed us all today
Love has made a circle
that holds us all inside
Where strangers are as family
and loneliness can't hide

    You must give yourself to love
    if love is what you're after
    Open up your heart
    to the tears and laughter
    and give yourself to love
    give yourself to love.

I've walked these mountains in the rain
I've learned to love the wind
I've been up before the sunrise
to watch the day begin
I always knew I'd find you
though I never did know how
But like sunshine on a cloudy day
you stand before me now

    So give yourself to love
    if love is what you're after
    Open up your heart
    to the tears and laughter
    and give yourself to love
    give yourself to love.

Love is born in fire;
it's planted like a seed
Love can't give you everything
But it gives you what you need
Love comes when you are ready,
love comes when you're afraid
It will be your greatest teacher,
the best friend you have made.

    So give yourself to love
    if love is what you're after
    Open up your heart
    to the tears and laughter
    and give yourself to love,
    give yourself to love.

    Give yourself to love
    if love is what you're after
    Open up your heart
    to the tears and laughter
    and give yourself to love,
    give yourself to love.

Desert Wind

Key: Am
No Capo

Words & Music
by Kate Wolf

Verse:

There's a wind_blow-ing down the can-yon so hot and dry,_ the rocks turn red. Shade

grows thin__ and shrinks to noth-ing as the sun_____climbs o-ver - head. What can I

Chorus:

say___ you said it all. Your words_ ride__ on the des-ert wind Tell-ing

me a-bout to - mor-row and how a heart__ can love a - gain.

There's a wind blowing down the canyon
So hot and dry, the rocks turn red
shade grows thin and shrinks to nothing
as the sun climbs over head

    What can I say, you said it all
    Your words ride on the desert wind
    telling me about tomorrow
    and how a heart can love again

Did you see the stars while you were sleeping
as they crossed the midnight sky

I could hear my own heart beating
in the stillness of the night

    Chorus:

It's all alone with the earth and sky
the hours are long, the days go slow
your lovin' way, like the wind reminds me
There is so much that I do not know

    Chorus:

    Chorus:

Green Eyes

Key: E
Capo: 4th fret

Words & Music
by Kate Wolf

Verse:

Ev - 'ry night we light_ the can - dle_____ that stands be - side our bed

Some-times the flame's too much to han - dle, that's what you said, that's what you said And you should know

Be-cause you built a fire_ in me____ and you made it burn, You fol - lowed me_ watch - ing ev - 'ry move, match-ing ev - 'ry turn. Your

98

Chorus:

green eyes they don't miss a thing,____ They

hold me like the sun____ go - ing down,_____

Warm me like a fire____ in the night,___ With-out a

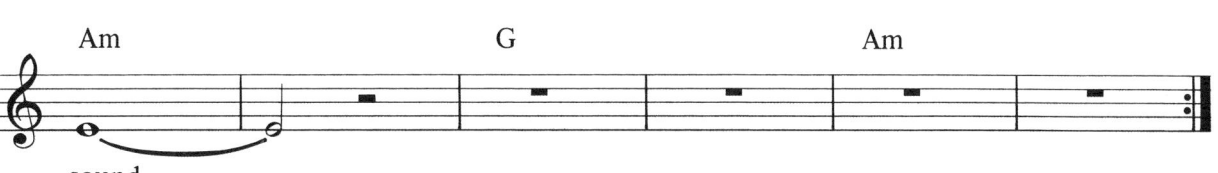

sound. . ._____

Every night we light the candle
that stands beside our bed.
Sometimes the flame's too much to handle,
that's what you said, that's what you said
And you should know..
Because you built a fire in me and you made it burn
You followed me, watching every move,
matching every turn.

    No, your green eyes they don't miss a thing,
    They hold me like the sun going down,
    Warm me like a fire in the night,
    Without a sound...

You were waiting 'till I heard,
just as patient as that lovelight in your eyes
You never threw away a word
or ever talked in a diguise

I ought to know...
You were a beacon to a sailor lost at sea,
I saw it in your eyes when you looked at me,
so openly

    Chorus:

The first time I ever felt your laughter
break loose inside and tumble out to me
My heart knew it had found what it was after
and it came so easily
We should know...
After all the years of the hard and lonely times
Now our days go by like best friends' story lines,
yours & mine.

    Chorus:

Hurry Home

Key: A
Capo: 2nd fret

Words & Music
by Kate Wolf

1. I wake up___and you're here be-side me   I fall a - sleep in your lov-ing arms You have

made   my life   so   hap - py   I count the min - utes when you're gone

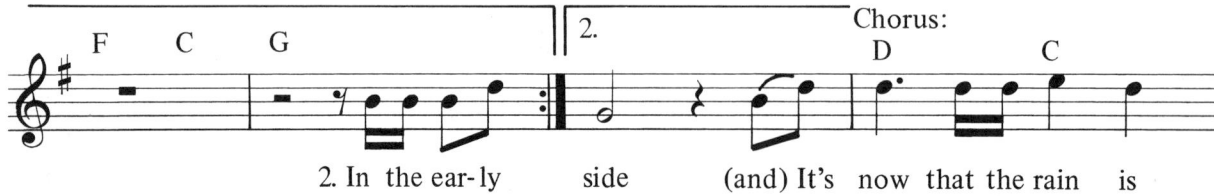

2. In the ear-ly   side   (and) It's   now   that the rain   is

fall - ing   and_   leaves_ turn red and gold   that I miss you   most_ can't you hear me

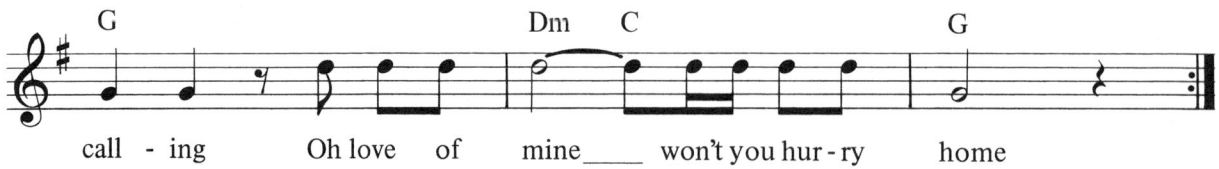

call - ing   Oh love   of   mine____ won't you hur - ry   home

I wake up and you're here beside me
I fall asleep in your loving arms
You have made my life so happy
I count the minutes when you're gone

In the early Spring we planted a garden
watched it grow in the summertime
Now the fields stand brown and empty
leaves blow down the mountainside

It's now that the rain is falling
and the leaves turn red and gold
I miss you most, can't you hear me calling
love of mine, won't you hurry home.

I will give you gold, I will give you silver
give you my word that this love is true
Give you anything just to make you happy
if I could spend my life with you

Chorus:
Chorus:

Kate and Odetta 1981

Cornflower Blue

Words & Music
by Kate Wolf

Key: E
Capo: 2nd fret

Corn-flow-er Blue,___ bloom-ing in the morn-ing sun

Tin-y flow-ers that grew from when our love had just be-gun___

___ Long a-go we plant-ed each

dry and dust-y row_____ How long it has tak-en_____

for the seeds of love to grow Corn-flow-er Blue___

Cornflower Blue,
blooming in the morning sun
Tiny Flowers that grew
from when our love had just begun
Long ago we planted
each dry and dusty row
How long it has taken
for the seeds of love to grow
Cornflower Blue

Cornflower Blue
like the faded shirt you wore
Standing in the shadows
when I opened up the door
The smile in your eyes
when you said hello

Held me tenderly
and would not let me go
Cornflower Blue

Cornflower Blue
deeper than the evening sky
Peaceful as a river
bluer than goodbye
Blue like the diamond
when the light shines true
If love came in colors
I'd choose this one for you
Cornflower Blue

Nina Gerber, Ford James and Kate

Far-Off Shore

Key: F
Capo: 1st fret

Words & Music
by Kate Wolf

Verse:

Watch-ing____ the sea 'till his days' work is done the

boat-man__ rows to the set-ting sun the

Catch-ing____ his oars in the sil-ver sea, he

leans on____ the wind as you lean on me.

Chorus:

Where the edge of the sea turns from blue to

green There's a far off__ shore that we've nev-er seen.

Watching the sea 'till his days' work is done,
the boatman rows to the setting sun.
Catching his oars in the silver sea,
he leans on the wind as you lean on me.

Where the edge of the sea
turns from blue to green
There's a far-off shore
that we've never seen.

When the moon comes up in your sea-green eyes
and we sail away in the deep dark night

I can't tell where you leave off and I begin
Love is just a way of breathing out and in.

Chorus:

So cast away and both shall row
there's no telling how long or where we will go
Rock on the water, race with the sun
Follow your stars as they shine one by one.

Chorus:

© *1981 Another Sundown Publishing Co. (BMI)*

Kate and Rose Maddox

These Times We're Living In

Key: G#m
Capo: 4th fret

Words & Music
by Kate Wolf

Verse:

Em ... D

Down by the riv - er the wa - ter's run - nin' low____ as I

C ... B7

wan - der un - der - neath the trees___

Em ... D

In the park out - side of town the leaves turned brown and yel - low now

C ... B7 ... Em

are fall - ing on__ the ground._ Re -

G ... D

mem-ber - ing__ the way you felt_ be - side me here when love was

C ... Em

new That feel-ing's just grown strong - er since I

D ... Em ... Chorus: ... C

fell in love_ with you. Now we've on - ly got these

106

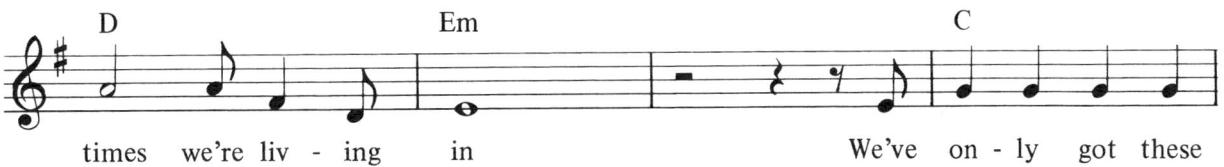

times   we're liv - ing   in   We've on - ly got these

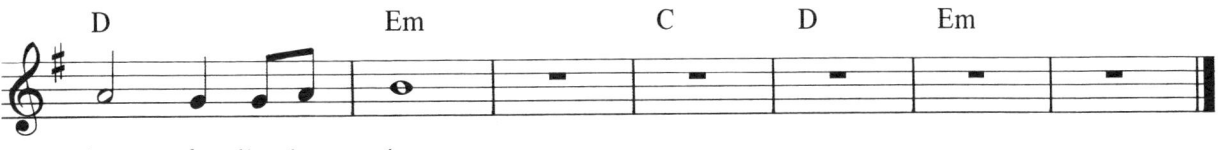

times   we're liv - ing   in.

Down by the river the water's runnin' low
as I wander underneath the trees
In the park outside of town
the leaves turned brown and yellow now
Are falling on the ground

Remembering the way you felt
beside me here when love was new
That feeling's just grown stronger
since I fell in love with you.

    Now we've only got these times we're living in
    We've only got these times we're living in

Winter wood piled on the porch
walnuts scattered on the ground
wood smoke risin' to the sky
An old man comes home from work
and hugs his wife in a sweatstained shirt,
steps through that door to where it's warm inside

And I'm walking as the wind
rustles in the fallen leaves

My footsteps picking out a tune
my heart sings silently

    How we've only got these times
    we're living in
    We've only got these times we're living in

See the roses dried and faded,
the tall trees carved and painted
With long forgotten lovers' names
The old cars standing empty
and dogs barking at me
as I walk through the quiet streets the same.

If I could I'd tell you now
there are no roads that do not bend
the days like flowers bloom and fade
and they do not come again.

    We've only got these times we're living in
    We've only got these times we're living in

Kate and Bruce Utah Phillips

107

Medicine Wheel

Key: G
No Capo

Words & Music
by Kate Wolf

Verse:

Em · D · Em

When the morn-ing breaks _ and the sun-light warms my soul

In the East the Ea - gle flies and the Red - tail proud -ly soars_

Em · G

____ I'm on my way to the place of the spir -it one__

Em · G

_____ Grand fa -ther hear me now____ I am on

D · Em

fire_____ Let the sun-dance guide my feet to your de - sire___

G · D

_____ Give me vi - sions for my eyes___ The

Am · D · Chorus:

words like gold_ that shim-mer in the sun Hy -

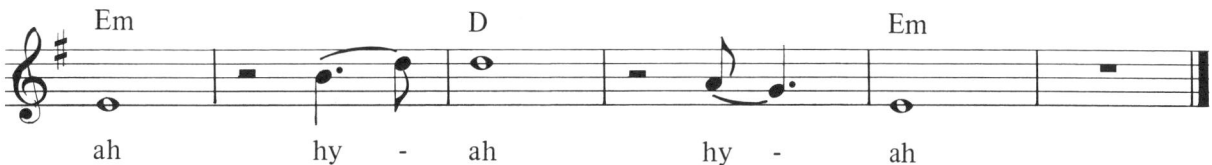

ah   hy - ah   hy - ah

When the morning breaks
and the sunlight warms my soul
In the East the Eagle flies
and the Red-tail proudly soars
I'm on my way
to the place of the spirit one
Grandfather hear me now
I am on fire.
Let the sundance guide my feet
to your desire
Give me visions for my eyes
and words like gold
that shimmer in the sun

     Hy-ah, hy-ah, hy-ah

When the sun goes down
and it grows too dark to see
I look within
to the shaman's mysteries.
I'm on my way,
to die and live again
Grandmother Earth I cry
give me rest.
I take my place with the
with the woman in the West
Show me the Raven and the Bear,
the way of herbs
and the black obsidian

     Hy-ah, hy-ah, hy-ah

Turn toward the South
like the water I will run
In innocence and trust
the moonchild's song is sung
I'm on my way
to the place of the sacred plants
My emotions and my will
at their command
Where the Turtle's voice
is heard upon the land
Where the wise Coyote prowls
the Rattlesnake will call me
to the dance.

     Hy-ah, hy-ah, hy-ah

In the deepest night
the stars watch over me
Old woman of the North
my mind seeks clarity
I'm on my way
to the place of the northern winds
Let the thunder and the lightning carry me
Lay my thoughts to rest
and send me into sleep
With the Hawk and the Buffalo
my dreams white crystal,
magic medicine

     Hy-ah, hy-ah, hy-ah, hy-ah, hy-ah

Kate's camp in the desert at Joshua Tree National Monument, 1982.

6

POET'S
HEART

Poet's Heart

Key: B
Capo: 4th fret

Words & Music
by Kate Wolf

Verse:

I wrote to you_____ some - where in south Aus - tra - lia A

po - et's heart in the eye of a hur - ri -cane____ I

strug-gle with find-ing words to sing these days, I said___ As

if my thoughts are wait - ing in the wings_____

for the stage to clear____ And you in your

el - e - gance and hu - mor fill the room__ your love and your con-cern_

Your an - ger at__ the in - jus - tice____ of

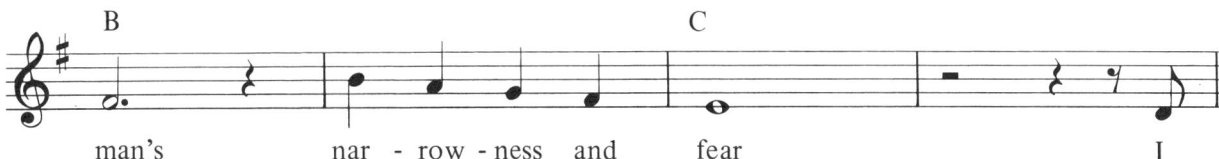

man's   nar - row - ness   and   fear   I

thank   you_   for   be -ing   here_

I wrote to you
    somewhere in South Australia
A poet's heart
    in the eye of a hurricane
I struggle with finding words
    to sing these days I said
As if my thoughts are waiting in the wings
    for the stage to clear

    And you in your elegance and humor
    fill the room
    your love and your concern
    Your anger at the injustice of man's
    narrowness and fear
    I thank you for being here

You wrote of love
    from the coast of Mendocino
A poet's heart
    crying a fighter's tears
The children of your body
    spread out across this earth
Like messages written across time
    measuring the years

    And you in your elegance . . . .

I heard your songs
    reach out to California
A poet's heart
    locked in the Coeur d'Alene
Of the old men and the booze,
    singing out the truth in lives
Of forgiveness and loyalties to friends
    constant as the endless railroad ties

    And you in your elegance . . . .

So here we are
    joined finally by our words
All poets' hearts
    close though far apart
I remember how you said
    that language is a knife
That spreads what we feel across the dry crust
    of someone's heart

    And you in your elegance . . . .

Kate with heart-shaped guitar by the late instrument maker Frank Gay-Edmonton, Alberta.

Carolina Pines

Key: G
No Capo

Words & Music
by Kate Wolf

Verse:

G **C**
Just an old house with the roof fall - ing___ in

G **D**
stand-ing at the edge of the field

G **G7** **C** **Cm**
Watch - ing the crops grow as it's al - ways done be - fore

G **C** **Em** **D**
No - bod - y lives here an - y more The

Chorus:

C **D** **G** **Em**
sun's go - in' down___ in the Car - o - li - na Pines I'm a

C **D** **G** **Em**
long way from home and I miss that love_ of mine

C **D** **G** **Em**
Bro - ken__ win - dows__ emp - ty doors, No -

114

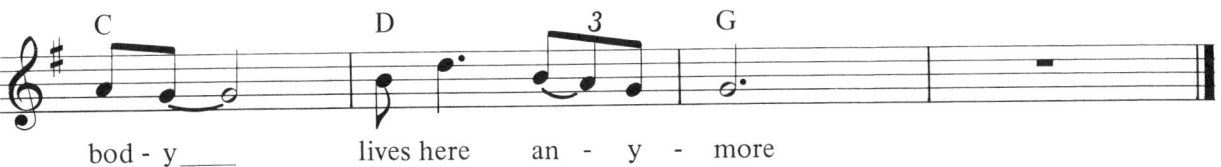

bod - y____   lives here   an - y - more

Just an old house with the roof falling in
   standing at the edge of the field
Watching the crops grow as it's always done before
   Nobody lives here anymore

     The sun's going down in the Carolina Pines
     I'm a long way from home and I miss that
       love of mine
     Broken windows, empty doors
     Nobody lives here anymore

Old memories come whistling like the wind
   through the walls and the cracked
   window panes

And the grass is growing high around the
     kitchen door
     Nobody lives here anymore

     The sun's going down . . . .

Once there were children and a few hired hands
     a hard-working woman and a bone-tired man
Now that old sun steals across a dusty floor
     Nobody lives here anymore

     The sun's going down . . . .

Muddy Roads

Key: D
No Capo

Words & Music
by Kate Wolf

Verse:

D   G   A   G   D

If I claim to have the an - swers   would I be tak - ing chan-ces, Lov-ing

A   D   G   A

you?   And if   I   could say   the   wind   was   right__

G   D   3   A   Chorus:

I should-n't stay with   you   to - night — Who would lose?   'Cause you

G   A   G   D

got me   danc - ing down these   mud- dy roads   with soft sand   be-tween my toes Feel-ing

A   G   D

__ fine   The sun - light_   play-ing   on   my   back

A   D

shirt in hand   Sing-ing out   in   cra - zy rhyme

116

If I claim to have the answers
    would I be taking chances
    Loving you?
And if I could say the wind was right
    I shouldn't stay with you tonight
    Who would lose?

        'Cause you got me dancing down
        these muddy roads
        with soft sand between my toes,
        Feeling fine
        The sunlight playing on my back,
        shirt in hand,
        Singing out in crazy rhyme

And if I could see around the bend
    would it change the time I spend
    Wanting you?

If I could bring you a perfect rose
    from all the pretty buds that grow
    How could I choose?

        You got me dancing . . . .

If I could count the days to come
    and mark them off one by one
    To spend with you
I'd be rich but never poor
    I'd find myself with many more
    Than I could use

        'Cause you got me dancing . . . .

Max Wolf and Kate

All He Ever Saw Was You

Key: G
No Capo

Words & Music
by Kate Wolf

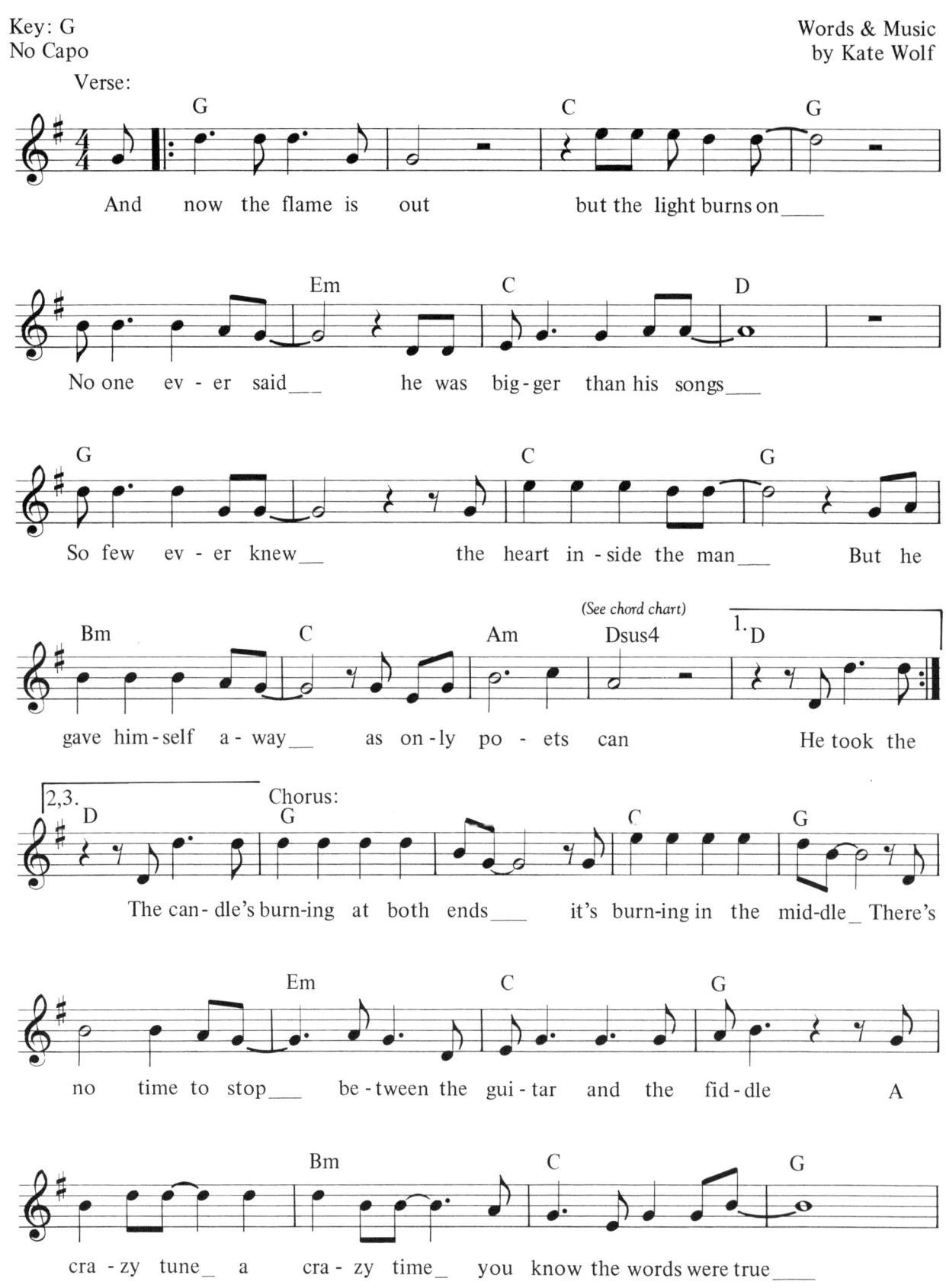

118

Smiles lit their eyes_ but all he ev-er saw_ was you

And now the flame is out
    but the light burns on
No one ever said
    he was bigger than his songs
So few ever knew
    the heart inside the man
But he gave himself away
    as only poets can

He took the stories of his people
    and gave them back in rhyme
But for the pleasures of the hearth
    there was never enough time
He said one day he'd quit
    and then he would come home
But there was always one more stage
    always one more road

The candle's burning at both ends
    it's burning in the middle
There's no time to stop
    between the guitar and the fiddle
A crazy tune, a crazy time
    you know the words were true
Smiles lit their eyes
    but all he ever saw was you

And the road finally claimed him
    like a sailor lost at sea
Setting sail on the horizon
    that would not let him be
Following a star
    that drew him like a flame
And 'though he loved you so well
    it was not the same

The candle's burning . . . .

Brother Warrior

Key: Gm
Capo: 3rd fret

Words & Music
by Kate Wolf

Gen-tle war - rior with your heart like gold and a rain-bow in your eyes Brave com-

pan - ion do you see a world shin - ing in the sky With your

bod - y danc-ing like an ar - row_ spread-ing joy be - neath your

feet And your hands that wave like tall_ grass in the

wind as you speak With the shy - ness of a

small child and the wis - dom_ of a sage I tell_ you now

_ there is no rea - son_ to be a - fraid

120

Gentle warrior,
  with your heart like gold
  and a rainbow in your eyes.
Brave companion,
  do you see a world
  shining in the sky?
With your body dancing like an arrow,
  spreading joy beneath your feet,
And your hands that wave like tall grass
  in the wind as you speak.
With the shyness of a small child
  and the wisdom of a sage,
I tell you now, there is no reason
  to be afraid.

Brother warrior,
  there are none of us
  who walk this path alone.

Spirit healer,
  it's the only life
  that we have ever known.
I see your smile in the sunlight
  I hear your songs in the rain,
Hold you here inside me
  feel your love, and know your pain.
At this time when the earth is waking
  to the dawn of another age,
I tell you now there is no reason
  to be afraid.

We are crying for a vision
  that all living things can share
And Those Who Care
  are with us everywhere.

Crying Shame

Key: G
No Capo

Words & Music
by Kate Wolf

Verse:

G .... **C** ....

Two hearts, so much love to give_ a - fraid to lose so no -

G ....

bod - y wins Cry-ing at night for the touch of a lov - er when they

D .... **D7** .... **C** ....

fin - 'ly meet they can't touch each oth - er It's a cry - ing shame

G ....

1. 2.

It's a cry-ing shame It's a

C .... **G** ....

cry-ing shame It's a cry-ing shame

Bridge:

C .... **Bm** .... **G** ....

How it goes on - ly time will tell___ try for heav - en___ take a

Em .... **C** .... **D** .... **G** ....

chance on hell___ It's a hard way to learn the les - son of love that keeps the

122

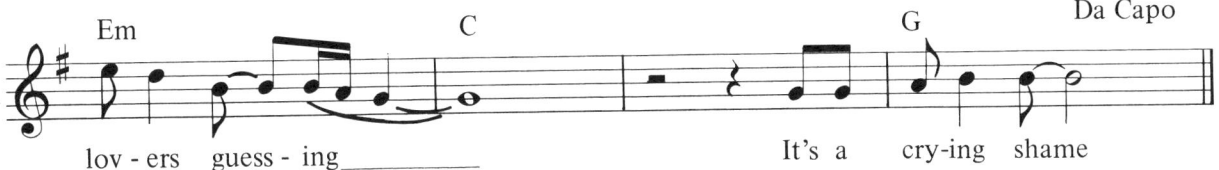

Em   C   G   Da Capo

lov - ers   guess - ing_____   It's a   cry-ing   shame

Two hearts, so much love to give
    afraid to lose so nobody wins
Crying at night for the touch of a lover
    when they finally meet
    they can't touch each other
It's a crying shame, it's a crying shame

Everybody sees it clearly
    how each one loved the other dearly
But they couldn't agree on what they had
    one called it happy and the other sad
It's a crying shame, it's a crying shame
    it's a crying shame, it's a crying shame

How it goes only time will tell
    try for heaven, take a chance on hell
It's a hard way to learn the lesson
    of a love that keeps the lovers guessing
    It's a crying shame

'Round and 'round the story goes
    it's play the game every gambler knows
Some get lucky, and they win
    some just lose again and again
It's a crying shame, it's a crying shame
    it's a crying shame, it's a crying shame
It's a crying shame, it's a crying shame
    it's a crying shame, it's a crying shame

Kate and Hannah Wolf

Slender Thread

Key: B♭
Capo: 3rd fret

Words & Music
by Kate Wolf

She's weav-ing him a pil-low full of dreams

soft win-ter wool and sum-mer fleece With the

col-ors_ of the ber-ries_ that grow a-mong the hills_____

Strands of cloud-y grey___ and deep blue in-di-go_____

And she sits be-side the o-pen door in the ev-'ning sun__

combs the card-ed wool in her lap her long hair all un-done

___ Talk-ing to the one___ she loves as she

weaves the hand-spun yarn___ like a web a-round her there to

keep her safe_ from harm___ She danc-es in his

heart like a feath-er_____ So fine the threads that

bind the souls to geth - er_____ She's weav-ing him a

pil - low for his head Some - times the strong-est love___

___ hangs____ by such a slen - der thread___

She's weaving him a pillow full of dreams
        soft winter wool and summer fleece
With the colors of the berries
        that grow among the hills
Strands of cloudy gray and deep blue indigo

And she sits beside the open door
        in the evening sun
        combs the carded wool in her lap,
        her long hair all undone
Talking to the one she loves
        as she weaves the hand-spun yarn
        like a web around her there
        to keep her safe from harm

            She dances in his heart like a feather
            So fine the threads that bind the souls
            together

She's weaving him a pillow for his head
Sometimes the strongest love hangs
        by such a slender thread

He always loved to sing those country songs
        about his mountain home and love gone
        wrong
That one about an old friend
        riding with the highway signs
But his favorites were the ones
        he could play between the lines.

He would sit on her porch in the evening light
        with his guitar in his hands singing to the
        night
Weaving pictures in her mind
        with every single word
        but the songs he wrote for her
        were the only ones she heard.

            She had his drifter's heart on a tether
            So fine the thread that bound the souls
            together

She loved to hear him sing that's what she said
Sometimes the strongest love hangs by such a
        slender thread

See him lying there with broken bones
        and a child's smile on a man full grown
If he'd gone just another inch
        by now he would be dead
At times a life can hang by such
        a slender thread

He can only thank his stars for another day
        and then he has to choose to live another
            way
But he can't ask her how this time,
        she's already said
        that fine line that you walk
        is just a slender thread

            She knows his heart
            can be as tough as leather
            So strong the threads that bind the souls
            together

But still he counts the scars inside his head
Sometimes the strongest love hangs by such a
        slender thread

She's weaving him a pillow for his head

Bill Griffin, Mike Auldridge, Kate and Pete Kennedy

In China Or A Woman's Heart
(THERE ARE PLACES NO ONE KNOWS)

Key: Bb
Capo: 3rd fret
Verse:

Words & Music
by Kate Wolf

She got it from her cap - tain when he sailed a - round the horn

Bring - ing gifts from Chi - na to their O - kla - ho - ma home. There were

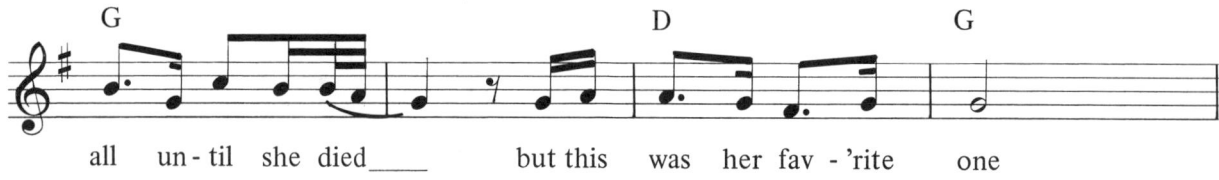

fan - cy silks and carved wood chests from the pla - ces he had gone — She kept them

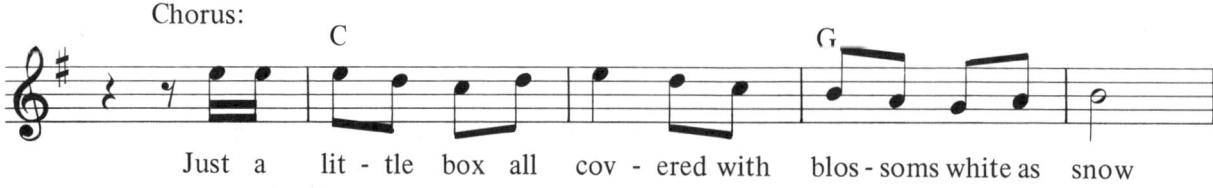

all un - til she died____ but this was her fav - 'rite one

Chorus:

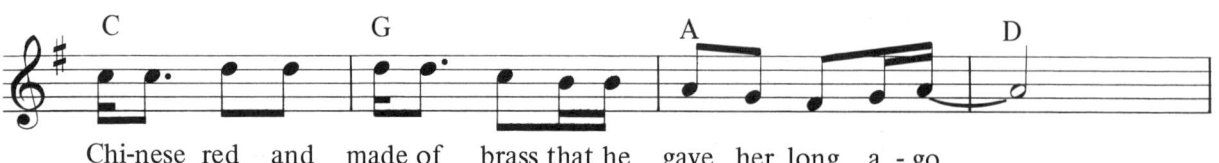

Just a lit - tle box all cov - ered with blos - soms white as snow

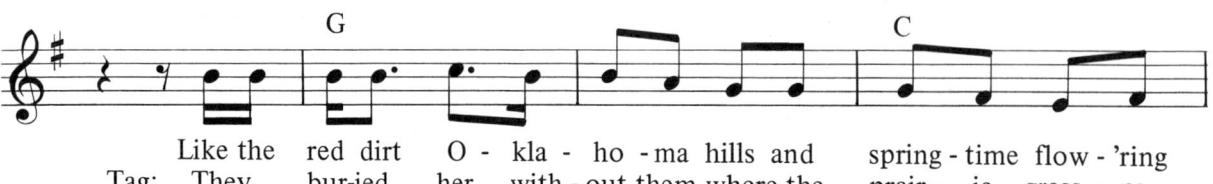

Chi - nese red and made of brass that he gave her long a - go_____

Like the red dirt O - kla - ho - ma hills and spring - time flow - 'ring
Tag: They bur - ied her with - out them where the prair - ie grass - es

trees   That she kept with all the love they shared in-side her mem- o - ries.
grow   In__ Chin - a or   a wom-an's heart there are pla-ces no one   knows.

She got it from her captain
    when he sailed around the horn
Bringing gifts from China
    to their Oklahoma home
There were fancy silks and carved wood chests
    from the places he had gone
She kept them all until she died
    but this was her favorite one

    Just a little box all covered
    with blossoms white as snow
    Chinese red and made of brass
    that he gave her long ago
    Like the red dirt Oklahoma hills
    and the springtime flowering trees
    That she kept with all the love they shared
    inside her memories

She kept it on her dresser
    filled with gold and silver rings
Necklaces of turquoise
    beads and other things
It filled her heart with the mystery
    and the magic of the day
When he gave it to her for her own
    in his quiet loving way

Ten years they spent together
    he'd come home and then he'd leave
And one day while she waited
    he disappeared at sea
No one knew how she'd call his name
    to the silent rocks and stones
Or how she'd sit and hold that little box
    so she would not feel alone

    Just a little box all covered . . . .

She never was a dancer
    or wrote a fancy line
The treasures of her life
    were the things she left behind
They buried her without them
    where the prairie grasses grow
In China or a woman's heart
    there are places no one knows

    Just a little box all covered . . . . . .

They buried her without them
    where the prairie grasses grow
In China or a woman's heart
    there are places no one knows

See Here, She Said

Words & Music
by Kate Wolf

Key: A
No Capo

The sun is sink - ing in the sea___ as she sings my life for me__

A tap - es - try of chil-dren's smiles wrapped in mem-o - ries and miles

last time to ⊕ Coda

You'd bet-ter do the things you dream see here, she said you know it seems That

chil-dren grow and lov-ers sleep and the time that's left is yours to keep

⊕ Coda

Pic-tures on - ly I can see_ songs that sleep in - side of me_ See here

__ she said_ you must be-lieve___ see here_ she said_ you know it seems that

(Resolves to A)

chil-dren grow and lov-ers sleep and the time that's left is yours to keep

The sun is sinking in the sea
    as she sings my life for me
A tapestry of children's smiles
    wrapped in memories and miles
You'd better do the things you dream
    see here, she said, you know it seems
That children grow and lovers sleep
    and the time that's left is yours to keep

Her song rises like the wave
    then falls and takes me far away
A sorceress on hammered keys
    her fingers play my destiny
See here, she said, you must believe
    see here, she said, look at your dreams
'Cause children grow and lovers sleep
    and the time that's left is yours to keep

It tears from her like a cry
    then soothes me like a lullaby
I can see her sing through half closed eyes
    see here, she said, dreams never lie
My dreams are visions on the wind
    and places I have never been
Pictures only I can see,
    songs that sleep inside of me
See here, she said, you must believe
    see here, she said, look at your dreams
'Cause children grow and lovers sleep
    and the time that's left is yours to keep

GUITAR CHORD CHART

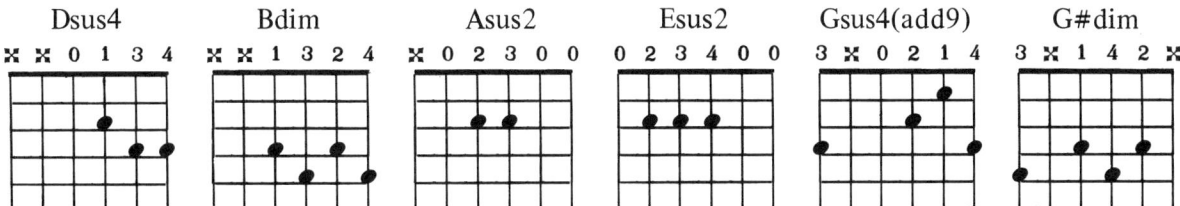

Dsus4   Bdim   Asus2   Esus2   Gsus4(add9)   G#dim

DISCOGRAPHY

All songs written by Kate Wolf unless otherwise noted (   )
All songs written by Kate Wolf are published by Another Sundown Publishing Company (BMI)

WE WALKED BY THE WATER
Sociologically Singing Volume 6
1973 Shoostryng Records
Lionel Kilberg and Kate Wolf with Don Coffin
Lyrics by Lionel Kilberg
Music by Kate Wolf

We Walked By The Water
Equality
Liberation
I'm 82
Help
You

Breezes
Nevada
You Can't Go Back
There Are No Medals For Loneliness
It Only Takes
Sonja Fromerova

BACK ROADS
1976 Owl Records OL-001
Re-released as Kaleidoscope Records F-6

Lately
Emma Rose
Sitting On The Porch
The Redtail Hawk (George Schroder)
Telluride (David West & Cyrus Clarke)
Goodbye Babe
It Ain't In The Wine (Lee Greenwood)
Tequila & Me
Legend In His Time (David West & Cyrus Clarke)
Riding In The Country
Oklahoma Going Home
Back Roads

LINES ON THE PAPER
1977 Owl Records OL-003
Re-released as Kaleidoscope Records F-7

I Don't Know Why
Lines On The Paper
You're Not Standing Like You Used To
Picture Puzzle
The Heart
The Trumpet Vine
I Never Knew My Father
Amazed To Find
Everybody's Looking For The Same Thing (Kate Wolf
    & Hugh Shacklett)
The Lilac And The Apple
Midnight On The Water (Traditional. Lyrics by
    John Croizat)
Lay Me Down Easy

THE PHILADELPHIA FOLK FESTIVAL
1978 Flying Fish Records FF-064
(A collection of recordings made by individual artists
at the 1977 Philadelphia Folk Festival)

Then Came The Children (Siebel)

SAFE AT ANCHOR
1979 Kaleidoscope Records F-11

Safe At Anchor
Early Morning Melody
Sweet Love
She Rises Like The Dolphin
Great Love Of My Life
Shining!
September Song
Seashore Mountain Lady
Looking Back At You
Two-Way Waltz

CLOSE TO YOU
1981 Kaleidoscope Records F-15

Across The Great Divide
Leggett Serenade
Like A River
Unfinished Life
Friend Of Mine (Kate Wolf, Nina Gerber &
   Ford James)
Love Still Remains
Eyes Of A Painter
Here In California
Stone In The Water
Close To You

FIRST PRESS
1981 Rail Records #101
(This compilation of Sonoma, California artists
includes one song written and recorded by Kate)

Although I've Gone Away

(Recorded live at the Great American Music Hall,
San Francisco; the Veteran's Memorial Building,
Davis; the American Victorian Museum, Nevada
City. *Medicine Wheel* and *Far-Off Shore* recorded at
Arch Studios, Berkeley, California.)

GIVE YOURSELF TO LOVE
1983 Kaleidoscope Records F-3000

Give Yourself To Love
Desert Wind
Peaceful Easy Feeling (Jack Tempchin)
The Ballad Of Weaverville (Jim Ringer &
   Mary McCaslin)
Green Eyes
You're Not Standing Like You Used To
The Hobo (Hugh Shacklett)
Hurry Home
Some Kind Of Love (John Stewart)
Who Knows Where The Time Goes (Sandy Denny)
Cornflower Blue
Picture Puzzle
Far-Off Shore
Agent Orange (Muriel Hogan)
These Times We're Living In
Sweet Companion (John McNicholas)
Medicine Wheel
Pacheco (Robin Williamson)
The Redtail Hawk (George Schroder)
Friend Of Mine (Kate Wolf, Nina Gerber &
   Ford James)

OUT OF THE DARKNESS
1984 Fire On The Mountain 4001
(Kate recorded one song for this collection)
The Sun Is Burning (Ian Campbell)

POET'S HEART
1985 Kaleidoscope Records F-24

Poet's Heart
Carolina Pines
Muddy Roads
All He Ever Saw Was You
Brother Warrior
Crying Shame
Slender Thread
In China Or A Woman's Heart
   (There Are Places No One Knows)
See Here, She Said

GOLD IN CALIFORNIA
A Retrospective Of Studio Recordings 1975-1985
(Compiled by Kate Wolf)
1986 Kaleidoscope Records F-3001

Full Time Woman (Alice Stuart)
She Rises Like The Dolphin
Like A River
Telluride (David West & Cyrus Clarke)
Muddy Roads
Across The Great Divide
The Lilac And The Apple
Unfinished Life
Early Morning Melody
Safe At Anchor
The Redtail Hawk (George Schroder)
The Sun Is Burning (Ian Campbell)
Brother Warrior
Two-Way Waltz
Eyes Of A Painter
Emma Rose
Here In California
Poet's Heart
Carolina Pines
The Trumpet Vine

THE WIND BLOWS WILD
A Collection Of Studio Recordings,
Radio Shows And Live Performances
(Compiled by Nina Gerber)
1989 Kaleidoscope Records F-30

Old Jerome
Statues Made Of Clay
Monday In The Mountains
Laugh Like That
Rising Of The Moon
Streets Of Calgary
Fly Away
The Wind Blows Wild
Clearing In The Forest (Utah Phillips)
Give Yourself To Love

AN EVENING IN AUSTIN
Recorded Live November 1985 On Austin
City Limits, Austin, Texas
1989 Owl Productions Owl-005 Videocassette
1989 Kaleidoscope Records K-36 Soundtrack

Eyes Of A Painter
Green Eyes
Picture Puzzle
Brother Warrior
Carolina Pines
Crying Shame
Love Still Remains
Like A River
Give Yourself To Love
Pacheco (Robin Williamson)
The Redtail Hawk (George Schroder)
These Times We're Living In
Let's Get Together (Dino Valenti)
Friend Of Mine (Kate Wolf, Nina Gerber &
    Ford James)
One More Song (Jack Tempchin)

Restored to original full length 75 minutes,
remastered and remixed by Max Wolf, Nina
Gerber and Tom Diamant.

Kate also performed on numerous friends' recordings including:

Peter Allsop
Draw The Line
1979 Flying Fish Records FF-223

Rick Byars with Eddie B. Barlow
Fallin' In Love Everyday
1979 Merrell Records MR-001

Chris Caswell & Danny Carnahan
New Leaves On An Old Tree
1981 Kicking Mule Records KM-313

The Perfect Crime: Hugh Shacklett & John Brandeburg
Recorded 1981. As yet unreleased.

Terry Garthwaite
Moving Day
1984 Catero Records CAT-007

Tony Rice
Cold On The Shoulder
1984 Rounder Records 0183

ALPHABETICAL
INDEX